DATE DUE

JAN 2 9 2008	
FEB 1 1 2011	

BRODART, CO.   Cat. No. 23-221-003

"Jeffrey Pfeffer has a rare combination of academic rigor and practical genius. Grounded in research, a revered pioneer in his field—yet dedicated to helping leaders lead—he stands as one of the sparkling gems in the field of management."

—Jim Collins, author, *Good to Great*, and coauthor, *Built to Last*

"I work with real executives every day. An executive is seldom a God, Devil, Genius, or Idiot; an executive, like the rest of us, is a human being. *What Were They Thinking?* clearly explains why executives make human mistakes and how these common mistakes can be avoided. You may well think of your own mistakes and answer the question, 'What was *I* thinking?'"

—Marshall Goldsmith, executive coach and author, *What Got You Here Won't Get You There*

"A wise book of penetrating intellect wrapped in readable prose that every student, practitioner, and even expert in business must read. If they don't, it is their grand omission."

—Jack Valenti, Former President, Motion Picture Association of America

"Jeffrey Pfeffer is one of the leading organizational behavior scholars of our time. *What Were They Thinking?* provides an accessible and insightful integration of theory and pragmatism developed through the thoughtful lens that only Jeff could provide. You will consume this book like a good Chinese dinner—pick what you want to eat from a rich menu, and expect to be hungry for more in a few hours."

—Gary Loveman, Chairman, President, and CEO, Harrah's Entertainment, Inc.

"I can think of no scholar who has done more than Jeffrey Pfeffer to document how much a company's success depends on how well that company leverages the strength of its human resources. In *What Were They Thinking?*, Pfeffer provides numerous examples of the companies that get it wrong and the companies that get it right. The result is a theoretically grounded, practical guide for managers on how they can get the most from their people."

— Joel M. Podolny, Dean and William S. Beinecke Professor of Management, Yale School of Management

"Beyond *Managing with Power*, beyond *Hard Facts*, this latest book from Jeffrey Pfeffer takes the principle of "learning from the mistakes of others" and helps put it into applied practice for business leaders. Combining solid theory with plenty of practical examples, he relates cautionary tales of situations where short-sighted managers have accidentally wandered off the path to success. This helpful book taps into the voice of experience so that we don't all have to learn these lessons the hard way."

—David Kelley, Cofounder and Chairman, IDEO

"*What Were They Thinking?* is a collection of snippets, most of which are good common sense. Yet, given how uncommon good common sense can be in corporations, this anthology makes for a very useful reference volume."

— Shona L. Brown, SVP Business Operations, Google, and coauthor, *Competing on the Edge*

What Were They Thinking?

What Were They Thinking?

Unconventional Wisdom
About Management

Jeffrey Pfeffer

HARVARD BUSINESS SCHOOL PRESS
BOSTON, MASSACHUSETTS

Library of Congress Cataloging-in-Publication Data
Pfeffer, Jeffrey.
  What were they thinking? : unconventional wisdom about management /
Jeffrey Pfeffer.
      p. cm.
   ISBN-13: 978-1-4221-0312-8 (hardcover : alk. paper)
   ISBN-10: 1-4221-0312-9
   1. Management. 2. Supervision of employees. 3. Leadership. 4.
Organizational behavior. I. Title.
   HD31.P3985 2007
   658—dc22

                                        2006100701

The paper used in this publication meets the requirements of the American
National Standard for Permanence of Paper for Publications and Documents
in Libraries and Archives Z39.48-1992.

Contents

1 What Were They Thinking?   1
Avoiding Common Management Mistakes

Part I: People-Centered Strategies

2 The Face of Your Business   13
*It's People, Not Software, That Build
Customer Relationships*

3 Making Companies More Like Communities   19

4 A Blueprint for Success   25
Spend More on Training

5 How Companies Get Smarter   32
Taking Chances and Making Mistakes

6 Why Employees Should Lead Themselves   39

Part II: Creating Effective Workplaces

7 Stop Picking Employees' Pockets   49
It Seldom Fixes Anything

8   Let Workers Work   56
    The Downsides of Having People Manage
    Their Own Benefits

9   Why Spy on Your Employees?   62
    Building Trust in the Workplace

10   All Work, No Play?   68
    Maybe Long Hours Don't Pay

11   Sins of Commission   74
    Be Careful What You Pay For,
    You May Get It

12   More Mr. Nice Guy   81
    Why Cutting Benefits Is a Bad Idea

13   Resumes Don't Tell   87
    Pick People for What They Can Do,
    Not What They May Have Done

Part III: Power Play
            Rethinking Leadership and Influence

14   The Courage to Rise Above   95
    Don't Be Afraid to Stand Out

15   Executive-in-Chief   102
    The Importance of Framing and Repetition

16 How to Turn On the Charm   109
    Building Influence Through Real Human
    Interaction for a Change

17 A Field Day for Executives   116
    The Benefits of Knowing What Your
    Organization Actually Does

18 The Whole Truth, and Nothing But   122

19 Refuse to Lose   127
    Persistence Pays

20 No More Excuses   133

Part IV: Measures of Success

Rethinking Organizational Strategy

21 The Real Budget Crisis   141
    Stop Rewarding Forecasting and Negotiating
    Instead of Real Performance

22 Shareholder Return Is the Wrong Measure
    of Performance   147

23 Dare to Be Different   154

24 Curbing the Urge to Merge   160

25 Don't Believe the Hype About Strategy   166

Part V: Facing the Nation
Organizations and Public Policy

26   In Praise of Organized Labor   173
What Unions Really Do

27   What to Do—and Not Do—
About Executive Pay   181

28   Stopping Corporate Misdeeds   188
How We Teach the Wrong Lessons

Notes   195
Index   213
Acknowledgments   239
About the Author   243

CHAPTER 1

What Were They Thinking?
Avoiding Common Management Mistakes

LEADERS OF COMPANIES and, for that matter, nonprofits and government agencies and departments face a number of challenges. First of all, in confronting high-stakes situations with substantial economic consequences, senior executives need to make numerous decisions about how to hire and obtain the discretionary effort of employees, how to compete, how to lead, how to deal with various external constituencies and policy issues, how to best manage their own careers—basically, to figure out "what works" and what to do about a number of important issues. Second, today's managers often need guidance and advice in figuring out what to do but can't—or won't—spend lots of time reading long treatises on each of these topic domains. And third, if and when companies follow prevailing conventional wisdom, they often discover, if they are attentive, that much of that conventional wisdom is wrong or misleading.

Beginning in January 2003, I have written monthly columns for *Business 2.0*, a Time Warner business magazine, that appear in the "What Works" section. The columns have covered a broad range of issues, but have mostly focused on common mistakes I see in how companies manage their people and their business, and also on how to do things better. The columns cover many of the important topics and decisions—like those just described—confronting organizations of all types. The columns are only about 650 words long—a single page. That very tight word limit has precluded me from developing arguments and explanations as thoroughly as might be most helpful, putting in as much data as I would like, providing more examples and context, and, most importantly, having the space to explain not only "what works" but "why it works"—the logic behind the analysis.

Thus, the genesis of this book. I have taken some of those columns, combined some others, and in each instance have redone and expanded the arguments, examples, data, and logic to provide a concise yet comprehensive discussion of what I consider to be a number of the most important management issues and management miscues and triumphs. Because the chapters are each only a few pages, the reader doesn't have to commit to becoming an "expert" on a particular subject. To provide additional help to people facing the challenge of making important decisions in a welter of conflicting and often incorrect information, the chapters include some endnotes and ideas and data so that for anyone who wants to, it is possible to pursue each topic in further detail.

The chapters are designed to provoke reflection and thought. My objective is, as it is in most of my activities, to "educate" the reader. Education, as I have come to understand it during more than three decades as a business school professor, is not telling people things they already know nor providing them with ideas that they necessarily already agree with. Education is concerned with helping people see and understand things in different ways, getting them to question previously unquestioned assumptions and ideas, and mostly helping them think and ask questions to uncover some fundamental insights.

Although the chapters cover a wide range of management topics, as I wrote this book I discovered that common ideas appeared in many of the examples. So, to help the reader see what the various discussions of management topics have in common, let's consider the threads that run through most, if not all, of the discussions.

COMMON THEMES

Almost every day, sometimes many times a day, I read an article about some organization or see a company or its leaders in action and exclaim, "What were they thinking?" It frequently seems as if organizational management is something drawn from a *Dilbert* cartoon, except with serious consequences for both the companies and their employees. But organizational leaders are hard-working, serious people, often expending enormous amounts of time and effort trying to do a good job. The problem is not one of intelligence or effort. Why do so many companies and their managers do so many things that seem so incorrect? In the spirit of the quality movement that has taught us to look for the root cause of problems so they can be fixed at the source, it is important to see what mind-sets and behaviors underlie many of the difficulties organizations face.

There seem to be three themes that unify many of the ideas in the chapters that follow and that help explain how companies make poor choices: (1) the importance of considering feedback effects—the idea that actions often have unintended consequences; (2) the naive, overly simplistic, almost mechanical models of people and organizations that seem to dominate both discourse and practice; and (3) the tendency to overcomplicate what are often reasonably straightforward choices and insights. By considering these ideas and their implications, I believe it is possible to, in many situations, come to a better understanding of what to do and make sounder judgments.

Feedback Effects

Actions have consequences. Decisions have repercussions. When companies do things to people, those people react. In too many situations, problems arise when we don't think through the likely consequences, repercussions, and reactions. There are literally scores of examples in the chapters that follow and in daily life. Here are a few.

When many companies get into financial difficulties, the first thing they do is cut wages and benefits. Cutting labor costs by cutting the expense of employees ought to help the financial condition of the organization. But things often don't work out quite as planned, and the reasons for this can be anticipated.

When I teach executives, I sometimes run the following little thought experiment. I will go up to one and say, "Assume that you work in my company and that you are who you are—a competent, experienced, hardworking, intelligent individual, doing your best to do your job as you think you should. Now I come to you and say, 'Our organization has fallen on hard times—which, by the way, may be because of strategic mistakes you had no part in making—and in order to restore profitability and financial viability, we need to cut salaries and other employee expenses such as benefits, by about 25 percent.' How do you feel about this, and what are you going to do in response?" I have never once had an executive respond by thanking me for making the tough decisions required to keep the organization economically viable. Instead, I typically get one of two responses. The first, often communicated with a reasonable amount of anger and emotion, is that the person is immediately going to look for another job and leave. The second response, if I add that general conditions of the job market preclude such a move, is that he is going to withhold effort and ideas, cut back on what he does, and maybe even find ways of getting back at management by intentionally messing things up.

Note what cutting salaries does beyond the immediate benefits of reducing the wage expense. First, it drives people to leave. And who is most likely to be able to find another job? Usually, the best people—those who have the most skills, experience, and the highest levels of performance. As the best people leave, turning the company around becomes more difficult, because turnarounds require insight and skill, and both are being lost. Second, cutting salaries creates a desire on the part of those who remain to passively (by slacking) or even actively (by sabotaging) harm the company. Such actions, or inactions, obviously make organizational performance worse and improvement in results more difficult to achieve. As a consequence, companies frequently find themselves in a pernicious race to the bottom, to see whether or not they can cut costs faster than the unintended consequences of those cost cuts reduce subsequent organizational performance.

Or take another example. As I was writing this book, the Tribune Company fired the publisher of the *Los Angeles Times* for the audacity of refusing an order to sack a quarter or more of the newspaper's newsroom staff. Many newspaper companies seem to have an interesting take on competitive dynamics in the media business and the source of their success. Facing increased competition from alternative news sources, including television and the Internet, their typical response is to cut reporting costs and other editorial expenses. Having cut the number of people who gather and write the news, the companies still have to fill their pages. So, their actions leave them filling up their newspapers with items from standard sources such as news services that can be accessed online or articles from other newspapers.

Consider the *San Francisco Chronicle*, owned by the Hearst Corporation. A high fraction of the articles in the first two news sections of the typical Sunday paper (and many of the daily papers as well) comes from the *New York Times*. This raises the question of why one would buy a paper whose quality and uniqueness is declining because of inadequate investment in staff; why not just buy the paper from which the *Chronicle* gets a lot of its stories and which has invested in its own, unique news gathering and reporting? The point is that the more newspapers cut their quality, the less incentive there is for anyone to subscribe. So subscriptions fall, more cuts are made, and the death spiral continues, if not accelerates. The only thing that can possibly provide competitive advantage in a saturated media marketplace is the quality of the writing and the ideas. An undifferentiated, unoriginal product of low quality is not going to save any company in the newspaper, or for that matter any other, industry.

There are ways to consider feedback effects and their likely results before taking actions. Some sophisticated analytical methods entail building formal models; for instance, as is done in the MIT systems dynamics lab by people such as Nelson Repenning and John Sterman. But it doesn't require formal modeling or scenario analysis to spend some time thinking about the likely consequences of interventions and taking those reactions into account as companies plan what they should do.

A More Nuanced View of What Motivates People and Makes Organizations Successful

The second thing that seems to get companies into trouble is holding and therefore acting on naive, simplistic, and inaccurate theories of human behavior and organizational performance. Again, there are many examples in this book and even more in the world.

The prevailing view that seems to form the foundation for many interventions is almost mechanical—if you want employees to do something, they need either positive inducements, or threats or punishments, or some combination of these inducements. In the absence of some external force, it seems to be assumed that people would be inert, just like objects in Newtonian physics where a body at rest will remain at rest unless impelled by some force into motion.

But we know this view of human behavior isn't true and that incentives and punishments have numerous problems. The use of monetary incentives can decrease or undermine intrinsic motivation, as extrinsic incentives provide a way for people to make sense of doing something without their having to believe that they like it. The attempt to control people's behavior through rewards and sanctions can engender psychological reactance, a process in which people rebel against constraints on their behavior—and are driven to do the very things they have been constrained from doing. Incentives are often very blunt forms of intervention, so we sometimes get the behavior we have rewarded only to discover we didn't really want it. For example, school systems that reward teachers for improving student test scores have sometimes found that the improvement was achieved by various forms of cheating.

Our view of organizational success and where it comes from is also often equally simplistic. We venerate the lowest-cost organizations. We admire the largest firms. But in many industries, success goes to the companies that offer the best value proposition, not necessarily those with the lowest costs. For instance, in the grocery store industry, Whole Foods Market is more profitable than its competitors even though many aspects of its business model raise its costs. But people will pay more for food they actually want to eat. Similarly, in many industries the most profitable firms are not the largest. Toyota is only now on the verge of overtaking General Motors in sales, but it has been much more profitable for a while. Southwest Airlines has been consistently profitable but it is not the largest airline. And so it goes.

If companies act on the basis of simplistic and inaccurate theories of human behavior and organizational performance, their decisions will not be good ones and the results will be poor.

Companies that are serious about overcoming this problem can spend more time getting informed about the facts, about history, and about alternative theories of behavior. Yes, this requires an investment of time and effort. But some forethought and learning can prevent some expensive errors.

Sometimes the Right Answer Is Obvious

The third problem that seems to get companies into trouble is making things overly complicated. This may seem to be inconsistent with the preceding issue, but it isn't. The fact is that human and organizational behavior is often quite comprehensible and readily understood, but not by using many of the more conventional and well-accepted perspectives.

For instance, the norm of reciprocity is both a simple and powerful idea. It is simple because it means just that favors will be reciprocated and so, probably, will harmful actions. People try to keep their interactions with others in a sort of balance, and don't want to do things for others when those efforts will never be repaid. People are unlikely to be friendly toward those who are unfriendly toward them. The idea is powerful because reciprocity is virtually a universal human norm, found in essentially every society that has ever been examined.

Now consider how the norm of reciprocity might help companies make decisions about managing people. If a company provides training and thereby makes an investment in its people, those people will be motivated to reciprocate through loyalty and effort. If companies provide wages and benefits that are perceived as generous, as being more than what would be required by the market—what economists such as George Ackerloff call efficiency wages—people will be likely to reciprocate for this generosity through increased discretionary effort and enhanced attachment to those companies. And vice versa. Cutting training and cutting the deal offered to employees is likely to induce reciprocal diminished effort and loyalty on the part of those who see the exchange as unbalanced.

The message in these chapters is that we ought to think before we act, taking into account feedback effects and using the insights of not only the large body of evidence on behavior but our own common sense and observations. It turns out both common sense and careful thought are in short supply. But that means there are great opportunities for those people and organizations willing to spend the effort to get beyond conventional management wisdom.

A "User's Manual" for This Book

Many business books today have lots of pages to describe one idea. My objective has been to have lots of ideas per page, and a lot of different topics and insights collected for you in one place. Consequently, there is a very simple but important way for you to use this book. Decide what topic you are currently interested in learning more about, what are the most important decisions you face. Are you deciding about your benefits policies and thinking about reducing benefits to cut costs or off-loading a lot of the responsibility and decisions to your employees? Are you in the process of hiring someone and thinking about how to use background information to make that decision? Are you faced with the challenge of influencing others, and do you need to become even more effective at doing so? Are you wondering about all this emphasis on "maximizing shareholder value" and if stock price really is a good measure of company or management performance? Do you feel as if the budgeting process is keeping you and your colleagues from making sound business decisions? Or even if you are not an organizational leader, do you want to better understand how to think about some business issue in your role as an employee or a customer of a particular company?

This book covers a lot of topics, so begin by thinking about what you are most interested in at the moment.

Then, use the chapter titles and section headings to find the pieces that appear to be most relevant to your current problems or interests. Look at those chapters. Think about the arguments, ideas, and data. And then, better educated about the issues and maybe a little more insightful about how to think about them, go about doing your job better informed and stimulated to think differently about management topics. This book is *not* intended to be read in any particular order, or from cover to cover. You should follow your own interests in navigating the material.

This book is a collection of management insights and data designed to help you do your job more effectively, whether that job is leading a company; working in it; or being a better-informed observer of organizations, what they do, and how they might do it even better. But you should also know at the outset that the chapters aren't going to tell you specifically what you ought to do. Each person's company and circumstances are too different for these chapters to offer advice about what particular actions to take. My presumption is that the readers of this book are like most of the managers and employees I have encountered over the years—serious, hardworking, intelligent individuals who are well grounded in the particular circumstances of their company and industry and career. This book can help by providing some unconventional insights into common management topics and problems. And just maybe by doing so, the chapters can help you think differently and more clearly. That increased insight, coupled with your own experience and judgment, can make both you and your organization more effective.

Part I

People-Centered Strategies

CHAPTER 2

The Face of Your Business

It's People, Not Software, That
Build Customer Relationships

CUSTOMER SERVICE HORROR STORIES are legion, and my wife
and I have certainly had our share. Airlines are frequent offend-
ers. United Airlines changed the scheduled departure of a flight
to Seattle from 7 a.m. to 6 a.m., and I was never notified. I missed
the flight, took an Alaska Airlines flight instead, and haven't flown
United again on this route. Virgin Atlantic's check-in desk in San
Francisco, staffed by contract employees since 2005, refused to
solve a problem with a connecting flight to Denmark because we
had the temerity to fly on their code-share partner Continental's
ticket—we actually had to call Continental from Virgin's check-in
desk to resolve the problem and almost missed our flight. And
retailers—don't ask. It's difficult to find sales help in many stores,
and if you do, the odds of the employees being able to actually
answer your questions and resolve issues are almost infinitesimal.
As an old cartoon once lamented, if we supposedly live in a service economy, how come there is so little service?

These experiences and, more importantly, the systematic survey
data on customer service and its consequences ought to disturb

businesses because of the implications for companies' economic success. A 2002 Pew Charitable Trusts survey reported that 46 percent of consumers had simply walked out of a store during the preceding year after encountering bad service, with higher-income respondents (people earning more than $75,000 a year) particularly likely to walk out. Eighty-one percent of those surveyed believed the stores they were patronizing were cutting corners on hiring—only because they are.[1] In a 2005 survey of more than 2,000 consumers in the United States and the United Kingdom, 49 percent of respondents said poor service caused them to change service providers in at least one industry during the preceding year.[2] Poor customer service or product quality were the leading reasons why customers switched their choice of vendors, exceeding even price as the explanation for why companies lost customers.

A United Kingdom survey published in the spring of 2006 found that fully one-quarter of customer service experiences during the preceding year had been negative.[3] The same report noted that 65 percent of the people studied had taken their business elsewhere after a bad service experience, with more than one-quarter claiming that their business, once lost, would be lost forever.

Ironically, even as customers suffer poor service and abandon businesses in droves, the prevailing rule of thumb is that it's "seven to ten times more expensive to generate a new customer than it is to sell to an existing customer."[4] Meanwhile, books and entire consulting practices have been built on the importance and profitability of customer loyalty.[5] Talk about a knowing-doing gap: companies seem to "know" that customer loyalty is important but they don't "do" much, if anything, to act on that knowledge.

And when companies do decide to act to build stronger relationships with their customers, they mostly emphasize the wrong approaches, seeking their salvation in technology instead of in their people. What companies appear to be doing in an attempt to increase service and improve customer retention is investing ever larger amounts in customer relationship management and automated customer service *software*, even though it is far from clear that such actions are going to make things better.

CRM is the technology that tracks customer activity and tailors marketing pitches accordingly. Estimates of the size and growth of the CRM software market vary considerably, in part because of what specifically gets defined as being related to customer relationship management and whether it is just software or maintenance and services that also get included in the expenditure estimates. Nevertheless, there is little doubt that the investment in this technology is both substantial and growing and an important focus of companies' investments. The Gartner Group estimated that worldwide spending on CRM was already $23 billion in 2000 and would grow to $76 billion by 2005.[6] Another report forecasted compounded annual growth of 11 percent between 2004 and 2014.[7] Spending on CRM dominates investment in categories of software. Retailers are particularly enamored of CRM technology, with one survey in 2003 finding that already 65 percent of retailers had implemented at least one CRM application and some 80 percent of those surveyed saying that investments in CRM were a good way to build their business.[8] Ironically, much of the investment in CRM software has been oriented toward reducing the costs of servicing customers, not building new or stronger customer relationships.[9]

But before you can *manage* a customer relationship, you first need to build or create that relationship. And customer relationships are not really built by fancy data-mining and statistical-analysis packages that track people's behavior, nor by the now-ubiquitous automated phone systems that basically just irritate people. (The Pew Trusts study reported that 94 percent of those surveyed—virtually every single person—said it was "very frustrating" to call a company and hear a recording rather than a human being.) Rather, relationships and their quality are determined by what happens to customers when they actually make contact with the organizations that have so avidly sought their business through advertising and other promotions.

Call Southwest Airlines and instead of hearing a "menu of options" you talk to a real person, often on the first or second ring, who actually seems to enjoy his or her job, has a friendly attitude, and appears to be happy to provide information and try and sell you a ticket. Following the 2001 attack on the World Trade Center and the catastrophic fall-off in the economy and air travel, Southwest maintained its perfect record of *never* having laid people off. With adequate staffing levels of engaged and loyal employees, the company can actually serve its customers—what a novel idea. Maybe that's why Southwest is the only U.S. airline that has been consistently profitable over the past 30-plus years. About two decades ago Jan Carlzon led a remarkable turnaround of SAS, the Scandinavian airline, based on the powerful observation that customers' feelings about a company came from the myriad small, often short, interactions they have with the organization—checking in, boarding the plane, getting served a drink or a meal, calling a reservations line.[10] If a company doesn't get these small experiences consistently right, nothing else matters.

Interactions between companies and their customers are still, even in this Internet age, often conducted by, of all things, real live human beings. That's why successful organizations in industries such as airlines, hospitality, retailing, and financial services are relentless in their attention to hiring people who will fit into a service-oriented culture; diligent in inculcating—through extensive training—service skills and attitudes; and, most importantly, scrupulous in taking care of their people so they will feel good about and be proud of the company and want to deliver a great customer experience.

So maybe instead of splurging on automated phone systems and software to analyze people's buying patterns, or even on fancier robotic telephone answering technology, if companies want to invest in technology to actually improve customer service and retention they might be better served to first invest money in software that helps them hire better people who are more likely to stay. Unicru (now part of Kronos) and Kenexa, for instance, are both organizations that sell systems that not only automate the hiring process, thereby saving money through enhanced efficiency, but also offer predictive models to select employees who are less likely to steal, less likely to quit, and more likely to provide great customer service experiences. Widely adopted in the grocery industry by companies like Whole Foods Market and Raley's and by retailers such as Nordstrom and the home improvement chain Lowe's, the evidence is convincing that these selection systems reduce turnover and turnover costs and help select better employees.

For instance, one grocery store compared 756 employees hired using the Unicru selection system with 1,273 hired using the traditional paper-and-pencil tests and subjective interviews over a three-year period. Involuntary terminations were 44 percent fewer and retention was 35 percent higher for the people hired using the Unicru system.[11] Such results are not that surprising, as selection science has been a focus of industrial psychology for literally decades. When coupled with a system that matches hiring data to subsequent retention and performance so there can be ongoing statistical analysis, there is the possibility of steadily improving company-specific selection processes and learning from experience.

Bill Clarke, a consultant to retailers with over three decades of experience, has made this perceptive comment about the importance of people to delivering customer service: "Many years ago I worked with a retail CEO who had an interesting way of viewing the interaction between the customer and the sales associate. He referred to it as 'the final 3 feet,' or the distance between the customer and the sales associate during a sales transaction . . . This space is the most valuable piece of real estate in a retail company . . . In over three decades of consulting, there is one recommendation that never, ever failed, namely, *the answer is always on the sales floor*. Wars are won on the battlefield, not in offices and boardrooms."[12]

It should be obvious that building and maintaining customer relationships begins with the customer experience. And that experience depends mostly on the interactions with the company's employees, who truly are the "face of the business."

CHAPTER 3

Making Companies More Like Communities

IN THE SPRING of 2006, just about the same time that the film version of *The Da Vinci Code* was hitting movie theaters, I was spending three weeks at a business school in Barcelona. While there, I discovered some of the management secrets of Opus Dei, the Catholic society at the center of the book and movie's byzantine plot and the subject of a cover story in *Time* magazine. No, I did not see any albino monks, cilices, or dead bodies. Instead, during my time at IESE, a leading Spanish business school founded by Opus Dei in 1958 as part of the University of Navarra, what I mostly observed was great management. In 2006, the *Financial Times* ranked IESE as number four in the world in executive education. With about three-quarters of the student body in its full-time MBA, executive MBA, and execu-tive education programs coming from outside of Spain, IESE was competing with business schools in Europe and around the world. The school had recovered from some financial stringency about two decades earlier to become one of the financially strongest business schools in Europe and, in 2006, was conduct-ing teaching programs in South America as well as in Europe, Africa, and the Middle East.

As a university, IESE's success obviously depends on the quality and commitment of its people, but that just makes the school similar to many companies where the quality of human capital has become the most crucial factor in being successful. As I explored what made IESE an attractive place to work, numerous faculty and staff at both the Barcelona and Madrid campuses told me that what caused them to join and kept them at IESE was its caring culture. Something about the place clearly drew people to it, because individuals with law and MBA degrees had forgone what were undoubtedly more lucrative financial opportunities to work at the school, and most of these individuals were not Opus Dei members; many were not practicing Catholics.

Culture, of course, is a relatively vague term. To be more specific, I believe that a large part of IESE's success derives from a management approach that one often sees in companies on the "best places to work" lists. That orientation proceeds from the premise that the organization is a community, not just a nexus of contracts or a set of transactions between faculty and the school that employs them, nor a set of financial relationships between students and alumni and a school that seeks to extract as much economically as possible from their pockets in the shortest amount of time—the apparent orientation of many U.S. business schools.

What does "organization as community" really mean in practice? In a community, people take care of each other. So, for instance, at DaVita, a large kidney dialysis company in the United States, the DaVita Village Network collects money from teammates, matched by the corporation, to help out employees facing financial stringency because of their own or a family member's illness. If you listen to people who have been helped by the network, it quickly becomes apparent that it is not just the financial support, but the emotional support, visits, help with household tasks such as cooking, and friendship that make such an enormous difference during difficult times.

IESE also cares for its people, even visitors. When my wife, Kathleen, came down with a severe earache from flying with a cold, the dean, Jordi Canals, arranged for an appointment first at a clinic and subsequently with a famous ear specialist, sent an English-speaking employee in a taxi to accompany her to both appointments, and paid for the taxi and the doctors' visits, no questions asked. This was neither required by the terms of my visit at IESE nor even expected, and naturally earned the undying gratitude of both my wife and myself. For Jordi Canals and his goal of building a community, it was almost automatic to offer help to someone who was having difficulty, even if that individual was just a temporary part of the organization.

A community is concerned about the involvement and engagement of its members in its activities, and measures that level of involvement while trying to do things to ensure that people affiliated with the organization remain connected to ongoing activities and attached to the collectivity. At IESE, with an alumni base of about 27,000 that includes people who may have attended only short executive programs, there were approximately 19,000 participants in alumni events held all over the world during the 2004–2005 school year. Moreover, about 40 percent of IESE's alumni gave money to the school, even though there is much less of a tradition of private donations in Europe compared with the United States. An alumnus who attains an important promotion or position or accomplishes something noteworthy receives a personal letter of congratulations from the dean; about 50 such letters get written each week. At Southwest Airlines, not only do its more than 40,000 employees receive birthday cards from the company, but any significant life event, be it happy or sad, is acknowledged with a note, a call, or both from a senior manager.

A community cares enough about the welfare and well-being of its people to make the necessary trade-offs required to actually live its values. At IESE, there is great emphasis on ethics and values—not just in response to current news events about financial scandals and the resulting public scrutiny of business education—but because of the school's commitment to the personal growth and development—in all aspects of their lives, not just the intellectual—of its students. IESE has determined (and my colleague David Bradford, an expert in interpersonal dynamics, has concurred in this assessment) that in senior executive programs, enrollments much beyond 35 do not permit the kind of close personal interaction that is so helpful for personal growth and transformation. Therefore, the school caps enrollments in its most senior programs at 35, with corresponding and larger sizes for different programs depending on the level of the target audience.

These are big lessons for U.S. companies, which have long resisted allowing more of their employees' lives inside their boundaries and instead have often built more transactional, arm's-length relationships with their people. Although CEOs pay lip service to the importance of both customer and employee loyalty, they frequently overlook the importance of personal relationships and connections in building such loyalty, and they rarely consider the idea of doing more than what is expected for their people because they think it costs too much.

One notable exception is Ed Ossie. I first met Ed when he was president and COO of MTW, a company that had initially provided contract software services before evolving into a provider of claims and policy software for the insurance industry. Under Ossie's leadership, the company grew from about $8 million to $40 million in revenues in about four years and drove its turnover from an industry-typical 30 percent level to just 4 percent. The company was then purchased by The Innovation Group (TIG), a 1,300-employee, U.K.-based publicly held company that provides outsourcing services and software to the insurance industry worldwide. After the purchase, Ed became a member of the board of directors, head of the company's technology division, and head of its U.S. operations and a member of the executive team. Ossie contends that a lot of MTW's success was because of the culture of community he and his colleagues had created.

The creation of community began as soon as new employees joined the company. On the first day, new employees' spouses, whether male or female, would receive flowers and a message welcoming them to the MTW family. Every function and business meeting held on an annual basis included family members. Family members were welcome at the company's offices, within reason. The company experimented with running a concierge service; it also provided "road warrior" points to people who had to travel extensively—the employees and their families received gifts and points in recognition of the sacrifices demanded by the necessary separation. People could take an afternoon to attend their kid's soccer game, if they wanted to.

Ossie has tried to continue the sense of community at TIG, but it is more difficult in a larger company that is more geographically dispersed. One way of getting people to feel identified with each other and the company is to have them work on projects that require real interdependence, even if they are staffed across countries and time zones. Working toward a common goal is a great way of pulling people together. Ossie commented that the need to communicate in order to coordinate interdependent work creates "the dialogue or the knowledge that the other person is out there and they matter to your team."[1] Also, there are now newsletters and companywide messages on the intranet that provide information about what is going on throughout the organization. And the company encourages people to help each other travel to each other's countries as a way of getting to know both other people in the company and their cultures.

Managing companies as communities is effective for several reasons. First of all, people are essentially social, affiliative creatures who enjoy being with others. That's one of the reasons why prisoner-of-war interrogation often entails social isolation and why social ostracism is such a severe penalty at institutions such as military academies. Making sure that people's natural social inclinations are nurtured by the organization's basic management practices is simply consistent with fundamental human psychology and increases the satisfaction people feel from being at work and the strength of the social ties that help bind them to the company.

Second, building a sense of community helps overcome the pervasive sense of alienation and distrust so prevalent in contemporary workplaces. After rounds of layoffs and management distortions and lies, people feel that they have to watch their backs. That vigilance is psychologically tiring and stressful. In a place where people care about and for each other, not just in word but in deed, there will be more trust and less stress in the relationships between people and their employing organization.

Third, one of the major stressors in contemporary life is trying to balance work and family demands and negotiating the sense of divided loyalty that many companies now seem to generate.[2] Conflicts between family and work roles have been shown to lead to alcohol use, diminished job and life satisfaction, less career and family satisfaction, exhaustion, depression, and physical ailments.[3] Incorporating more of a person's life, including his or her spouse and children, into the organization; acknowledging that the person has responsibilities to people outside of the company; and trying to show sympathy and concern both for those others and those responsibilities are all actions that build a deeper and less "transactional" relationship between the person and the company as well as among coworkers. And incorporating more of the family and family relationships into work obviously also can diminish the conflict between work and family roles and the associated problems that arise from such conflict.

But building a company as a community is less about "best practices" and sending flowers or birthday cards, and much more about the nature of the relationship created by the company and its leadership with the employees. In this effort, values and beliefs loom large. Companies can—and do—copy methods and programs easily enough. But a way of thinking that creates deeper social ties is much more difficult to duplicate.

CHAPTER 4

A Blueprint for Success

Spend More on Training

MANY EXECUTIVES, particularly in the United States, seem to believe that the key to competitive success is just getting government out of the way—lower taxation, less regulation and bureaucratic red tape—in other words, letting businesses build their business. Of course, these same executives are not always completely consistent in their preferences about the role of government. So, for instance, the head of the Silicon Valley Manufacturing Group complained on a public radio program about the tax and regulatory burdens faced by the high-technology industry, but also virtually in the same sentence called for more government investment in education. The gentleman didn't bother to explain how one could have *both* smaller government and lower taxes and also more funding for education at the same time.

Three facts, not always fully appreciated or reflected in conventional wisdom and discussion, can help us understand the contemporary competitive dynamics that affect both companies and countries. The first is that the United States is actually losing its competitive advantage in world markets, even in high technology. For instance, in November 2004, the United States ran a record trade deficit of $5.8 billion just in advanced technology products, with a 12-month trade deficit of $36.9 billion for these same goods. At the same time, the fastest-growing U.S. export during 2004 was scrap and waste—*trash*.[1] While the average GDP per hour worked in Western Europe was about 30 percent lower than in the United States about 30 years ago, the gap is now only about 5 percent. An analysis by the *Economist* magazine reported that job growth, returns to capital, and productivity growth have all recently been about the same in the European Union as in the United States.[2]

The second fact is that if U.S. companies and the U.S. economy have any problems competing in global markets, regulatory and tax burdens are almost certainly not the place to look for an explanation. All the complaining to the contrary, regulatory oversight of U.S. companies has decreased dramatically, under both Democratic and Republican administrations, over the past decade and more. For instance, the workforce of the Equal Employment Opportunity Commission, the agency that oversees the prohibitions against discrimination based on race, gender, age, national origin, and disability, decreased from 3,390 people in 1980 to just 2,544 by the end of fiscal year 1998, with just 760 investigators available to cover the entire economy. Between 1990 and 2000, the number of people working for the Consumer Products Safety Commission decreased from 520 to 479, employment at the National Labor Relations Board fell from 2,263 to 2,054, and even the Federal Trade Commission barely grew—from 988 to 1,019 people—even as the economy expanded dramatically in both size and complexity.[3]

Similar observations apply to the tax burden faced by business—the facts are that business taxes have been decreasing over time. While in 1943 corporate income taxes comprised some 40 percent of all tax revenues, that percentage fell to just 6 percent by 1983 and currently runs at about 10 percent.[4] As a percentage of GDP, federal revenue from corporate taxation has fallen from

2.2 percent in 1998 to just 1.6 percent in 2005. According to a *New York Times* article, "By most measures, the corporate tax burden is lower in the United States than it is in the European Union or in Japan or most other industrialized countries."[5]

A variety of studies have come to the same conclusion: the factors that are often cited as diminishing global competitiveness—high taxes and regulation—just aren't the problems that most demand the attention of business and government leaders. Look at the countries that consistently score highest on surveys of global competitiveness. The World Economic Forum's 2004 study sought to judge countries on their all-around ability to succeed in the global economy. Finland ranked first for the third time in four years, with Sweden, Norway, and Denmark—Nordic countries with generally high tax rates, lots of government intervention in the economy, strong trade unions, and generous social welfare programs—also in the top six (the United States ranked second and Taiwan fourth in the study).[6]

Likewise, Harvard Business School strategy guru Michael Porter's global Innovation Index ranked the United States as the most competitive nation in 1995. But Porter projected that by 2005 the United States would have fallen to sixth among the 17 OECD member countries, trailing Japan, Finland, Switzerland, Denmark, and Sweden.[7] In fact, a Globalization Index developed by consulting firm A.T. Kearney ranked the United States *seventh*, behind Ireland, Singapore, Switzerland, the Netherlands, Finland, and Canada.[8]

Author and researcher Richard Florida has argued that the United States built the most powerful economy in the world during the past several decades largely by attracting the best human capital from all over the planet and being open to new ideas. Now, however, Florida's global creative-class index, measured as the proportion of high-value "creative" jobs in the total economy, ranks the United States eleventh, behind countries such as Iceland, the Netherlands, Belgium, Canada, and, once again, Finland.[9]

The third important fact is this: a country's, or a company's, competitive advantage in the current economy depends primarily on its people's skill, talent, and educational attainment—its human capital. A 2004 *Economist* study of the globalization of research and development reported that 70 percent of the 104 senior executives responding to the survey said that their companies already employed R&D talent outside of the country of their headquarters, and that 52 percent planned to increase their investments in overseas R&D. In explaining where companies chose to locate their overseas research and development activities, the survey results showed that "labour costs, the quality of local infrastructure, favourable tax regimes, and government incentives all play a role, but skills are the biggest magnet for R&D investment."[10]

Even as we know that the most valuable form of work today is knowledge work, and the evidence shows that company location decisions, both within the United States and globally, are affected by the quality of the locally available labor force, study after study shows the United States falling farther and farther behind in educating its workforce. Only about 70 percent of high school students graduate in four years with a regular diploma, and the graduation rate for minority students in urban school districts is much lower.[11] A 2006 Conference Board survey of 431 human resource executives concluded, "The future workforce is here, and it is ill-prepared."[12]

While 42 percent of students in China earn undergraduate degrees in science and engineering, the comparable figure for the United States is just 5 percent.[13] China, India, Japan, and Europe all produce more science and engineering degrees than the United States.[14] A 2003 report on mathematics literacy for 15-year-olds showed that the United States ranked 24th out of 29 countries. The countries that most studies find to be the most competitive in the global economy ranked near the top of the list of mathematical proficiency, with Finland first, the Netherlands third, Japan fourth, and Canada fifth.[15] A 2000 assessment of 15-year-old students' academic abilities reported that the United

States ranked 15th of 27 countries on reading literacy, 18th on mathematics literacy, and 14th in science literacy.[16] Another report found not only that U.S. 12th-graders scored only in the tenth percentile in math, but that the students ranked themselves first in their own assessment of their performance.[17]

Historically, immigration has filled the gap in skills and talent created by domestic educational failings and students' choices of academic major. But since September 11, 2001, the United States has become much less accessible to skilled immigrants, and anti-immigrant sentiment has been harnessed as a political issue. A 2004 report by the Council of Graduate Schools found that the number of Chinese students applying to U.S. graduate programs had fallen by 45 percent and the number of Indian students had shrunk by nearly 28 percent, although there was subsequently some recovery in these numbers as pressure from U.S. universities caused the government to become more accommodating in granting student visas.

The implications of these facts for companies and their leaders are clear. First, executives need to acquire a better understanding of the facts about competitive dynamics so they can use their energies to press for real solutions to the real issues. Instead of whining about taxes and regulation, companies need to press for investment in infrastructure, particularly educational infrastructure at both the elementary and higher education levels. Recent fiscal stringency in states such as California has resulted in higher education budgets being cut and access to junior colleges and state universities restricted; some students have actually had offers of admission withdrawn because of inadequate capacity in state colleges and universities. These policy actions broke an implicit promise of access to higher education for all those who were motivated and qualified. These are precisely the wrong decisions to ensure future economic success and competitiveness that depend on the quality of human capital.

Second, companies need to accept responsibility for some of the costs associated with their own employee training and development.

General Electric with its facility in Crotonville, New York, and Motorola with Motorola University are both justifiably famous for building effective management teams and achieving the benefits of total quality management by investing in staff development. Companies on *Fortune*'s best places to work list have outperformed benchmark indices financially and also are among the leaders in their investments in their people. The Container Store's employees average 162 hours of training a year. Textile manufacturer Milliken requires workers to participate in 40 hours of training annually. Men's Wearhouse sends its wardrobe consultants—its salespeople—to four days of training at Suits University and does a lot of follow-on training as well. At construction company TDIndustries, all employees receive 100 percent reimbursement of tuition, other fees, and books at any state-supported college.[18]

Systematic quantitative studies of the effects of company investments in training also show the positive benefits of these expenditures. One analysis of all evaluations of training programs from 1960 to 2000 found medium to large positive effects, with the size of the effects being either comparable to or larger than for other organizational interventions designed to improve performance.[19] Another overview, taking a human capital perspective, reported that training was one of the few factors affecting wage and productivity growth.[20] A large U.S.-based multinational firm that evaluated the cost-effectiveness of some 18 training programs found an average improvement in job performance of 17 percent, with an average return on investment of 45 percent for the managerial training programs and 418 percent for sales and technical training.[21]

These positive effects occur because training has a number of important benefits. First of all and most directly, when training is effectively organized and delivered, people learn skills and knowledge that enhance their performance and their companies' ability to compete. Investments in training people in quality processes, for instance, permitted Motorola to win the Baldrige quality award and to enhance its product quality and efficiency, thereby reducing waste in both materials and labor and improving profitability. Second, training represents a tangible investment in people. The norm of reciprocity almost always operates; thus, seeing that their employer has invested in them, employees are likely to reciprocate by investing in their employers. They can do this by working harder and also by becoming more loyal and less likely to leave at the first chance for better opportunities elsewhere.

Third, investing in people and building their skills and abilities raises their sense of their own competency and capability. To the extent people believe they are better prepared and more skilled, they will perform at a higher level simply because they have more confidence in themselves, including a belief in their ability to learn and develop that encourages further learning and growth. This latter result is certainly one outcome of the training provided by Men's Wearhouse. Retail workers are typically low paid and most often receive training only in how to operate the cash register and open and close the store, if they receive any training at all. By investing in its people and telling them, through those investments, that they are important, the company raises the self-confidence and self-esteem of its wardrobe consultants. This makes them more effective salespeople, as it is difficult to effectively sell merchandise in the absence of a sense of self-confidence.

The evidence is overwhelming. Bureaucrats don't determine the long-term viability of American businesses. Brainpower and skills are what matter, and nurturing the capacity for innovation and invention is not only a sound investment, it is essential for companies' success. My guess is that business executives will be disappointed when they realize that lower taxes and investments in educational infrastructure today mean companies will get exactly what they have paid for, or not paid for, tomorrow—and nothing more. And the same holds true for their own investments in their employees and their skills.

CHAPTER 5

How Companies Get Smarter
Taking Chances and Making Mistakes

COMPANIES ARE A LOT like children—none of them are born knowing all that they need to know, and relatively few are born really smart. Most acquire intelligence by learning basic tasks and skills, mastering them, and then moving on to learn more advanced skills that can be used on more difficult problems and tasks. It has become virtually axiomatic that to succeed over time, companies have to continuously innovate, learn, and improve how they do things. That's why there has been so much emphasis on innovation and learning in the management literature. On Amazon .com there are almost 1,000 entries for "organizational learning" and 11,925 for "innovation." Google has 802 *million* entries for the word "innovation" and 2.5 million for "organizational learning." And the pressures to continuously improve are why, at least for a while, companies embraced the total quality management movement and why organizations in the United States invest billions—some estimates are more than $80 billion—annually on training and education.

Of course, you already know all this. The phrases "learning organization" and "continuous improvement" have become virtually management clichés. Nonetheless, relatively few companies actually embrace the management practices that are required to help them get smarter. That's because some of the things they need to do to learn are counterintuitive—or at least inconsistent with conventional wisdom and common management practice. Consider the research of Amy Edmondson, a professor at Harvard Business School, and her colleagues, who studied how hospitals and their employees acquired and implemented new knowledge and techniques. Learning about new science and practice and mastering new equipment and techniques are fundamental to the practice of good health care, because medicine is always changing in response to new research, pharmaceutical products, procedures, and equipment. Moreover, this adaptation has to occur in complex settings where the consequences for failure are high. Edmondson's research also investigated how health care organizations drove mistakes and errors out of the system. In short, Edmondson analyzed how to build a real learning organization. What she discovered makes perfect sense, but only if you think about second-order feedback effects and adopt a more long-term view of building a successful organization.[1]

Should a nurse who discovers a problem, such as an unmade bed in a room about to receive a patient, just fix the problem—in this instance, make the bed? Or to take a similar situation in different context, should a software programmer facing an unexpected coding glitch just develop a "workaround" patch to keep the project moving forward? Not according to Edmondson. Taking individual responsibility and fixing problems might seem like a conscientious and good thing to do—the problem is fixed and no one else has to get involved. But that's the rub. Consider the consequences—unless the unmade bed is brought to others' attention, no one besides the nurse will know there was ever a problem and therefore there will be no effort to discover the root cause and fix it. And the same applies to the software project. If the root causes of problems are not discovered and remedied, the problems will almost certainly recur, and then other people will be faced with the task of fixing them. Organizational learning thus requires people to direct others' attention to problems so they can be noticed, diagnosed, and fundamentally fixed once and for all. Organizations seldom like "noisy complainers," to use a phrase I first heard from my colleague Bob Sutton. But such people are vitally important for the learning process as long as their complaints are substantive.

Edmondson's research also examines a second conundrum—what about the effects of removing layers of management and lots of managers, and instead putting people in self-managed teams and leaving supervisors with larger spans of control? Isn't it better to have fewer managers and a flatter structure? The answer, according to both Edmondson's research and the experience of Southwest Airlines as described by Jody Hoffer Gittell, is it depends on what the managers do. If they just give orders and assign blame if things go wrong, you're probably better off with fewer of them. But if leaders actually help people coordinate and learn, more are better.

Southwest Airlines actually has one of the higher ratios of supervisors to those being supervised in the airline industry, much higher than the ratio at American Airlines, for instance.[2] And the research on health care organizations also found that those that learned the best generally had a higher proportion of managers. At Southwest and in the best health care organizations, the leaders were spending time in the task of relational coordination. They were helping their employees learn, moving information across organizational boundaries, and essentially scanning the environment for common trends and themes, and then bringing that information to their people, who could collectively use it to enhance performance.

The problem with having fewer managers is actually quite simple: since people have been taken out of the organization, those that remain have more to do unless something has been done to decrease the total workload. And there are fewer people in the organization to ensure coordination, reflection, and learning. In order for leaders to act as coaches, there must be enough leaders to do the coaching. Just as coaches help their teams perform better by standing on the sidelines and providing perspective and information that players in the thick of things might otherwise miss, so in companies it is useful to have people whose job responsibility includes learning, coaching, teaching, and reflecting, or else those activities won't occur.

Here's a third puzzle that comes from Edmondson's research: if, when you entered a hospital, you had a choice of two wards, which would you choose—Ward A or Ward B, which has *ten times* the number of reported errors as Ward A? When Edmondson and her colleagues discovered that medical units with *more* reported errors, for instance, in administering medicine, actually had better health outcomes for their patients, they were genuinely perplexed. But their fieldwork quickly made sense of the apparent paradox. Medical units could have fewer reported errors for one of two reasons: (1) they actually made fewer mistakes, or (2) they made as many or even more mistakes, but had a climate of fear in which mistakes were covered up instead of acknowledged.

In the organizations Edmondson studied, the second reason seemed to prevail. The units with more reported errors were generally led by people who understood that in complex environments with difficult tasks, stuff happens. The best way to ensure that the same mistakes were not made again and again was to acknowledge them, try to figure out their root causes, fix those causes, and then continually repeat that process. So, for instance, if no one ever admitted to making a mistake in administering medicine to a patient, there would be no way to uncover whether the problem was physicians' handwriting, having similar-color pills placed too close together, insufficient instructions and record keeping, and so forth. In medicine, the motto "forgive and remember" is embraced. Forgiveness is important for ensuring that people are willing to admit when they messed up, and remembering, particularly if that memory gets institutionalized in better work processes, is essential for preventing the same mistake from occurring again. Both uncovering mistakes and learning from them are essential for the learning process.

There are two other things that companies need to do to get smarter that are also contrary to common practice. The first is letting people do new things, a decision that often has costs in terms of short-term efficiency. It is obvious that learning at the level of the individual involves a certain amount of beginner's clumsiness—whether one is learning how to play a musical instrument, speak a new language, or make investment decisions. The irony is that even as companies want to become learning organizations, they don't want to be places where people can learn new things—because that requires putting people in positions where they do tasks they don't yet do very well.

At AES, the global independent power producer, people historically had the opportunity to volunteer for tasks such as deciding with teammates about health insurance plans or even, in the case of the company's Connecticut plant, having front-line employees invest about $10 million in reserves. The consequence was that people learned new skills. And there was a consequence for the company as well. After a while, people who have developed expertise become trapped in their accustomed way of doing things and by their existing knowledge, so having different people do the tasks brings fresh eyes to the problem.[3] Studies of innovation have found that much invention entails taking ideas and technologies from one context and using them in a different product or service environment, or combining existing elements in new ways and new settings.[4] Thus, companies can get smart when they encourage such internal knowledge brokering, something that is accomplished by having teams of people do different things.

Learning and innovation also require letting people make mistakes. Individuals inexperienced in doing some new task are obviously likely to make more errors than those with more experience. This is true even in the case of medicine. Doctors in training learn by doing, and often these initial efforts are not particularly skilled.[5] New procedures that will eventually save many lives, such as open heart surgery, and new devices such as stents, initially result in relatively high rates of mortality and morbidity until they are perfected through learning and experience. So, even in the highest-stakes situations, there seems to be no complete substitute for learning by doing and experimenting.

At the company level, bringing new products to market is obviously risky—some offerings will fail due to insufficient demand. The idea of running small experiments, a managerial practice embraced as a management mantra at Harrah's Entertainment, Yahoo!, and IDEO, takes into account that some of the experiments and innovations won't work, some of the Web site trials won't improve things, and some of the product prototypes will fail. Harrah's tries different ways of getting loyal players back into its properties, and not every idea is going to be equally successful. IDEO may make hundreds of prototypes for new toys, of which relatively few get tested in the marketplace and even fewer are ultimately successful.

IDEO's idea is that failing early and failing often is better than failing once, failing at the end, and failing big. The principle is simple—learn and fail on a small scale. But that ethos requires accepting that novelty and innovation are invariably accompanied by setbacks and failures. And embracing such a way of operating requires letting people fail—maybe even encouraging them to fail. After all, if nothing ever goes wrong, it must be because the capabilities of the system and its people have not been truly tested. This is a principle of total quality management—removing waste and inventory to highlight bottlenecks and problems that can then be fixed—in the process using problems and failures to highlight opportunities for improvement.

I've noticed that companies pay lip service to getting smarter but few do what is required to accomplish that lofty goal. Organizational learning requires three things: a clear understanding of recurring problems, the willingness to allocate resources to address the root causes of those problems, and cultural values that foster learning—which means encouraging employees to find, fix, and report mistakes rather than heroically patch things up. None of this may seem sexy or glamorous, and a lot of what is required seems to go against common sense ideas of "soldiering on," efficiency, and holding people personally accountable for every error. But if you really want to outsmart your competition, it's the only intelligent way to go.

CHAPTER 6

Why Employees Should Lead Themselves

THE ORPHEUS CHAMBER ORCHESTRA, headquartered in New York City, is justly famous for the musical accomplishments of its 27 permanent members and the other musicians who fill in as needed. The orchestra has won a Grammy Award and performs a broad repertoire of classical music—ranging from Bach to Schönberg—to rave reviews worldwide. The group is also famous—it has been written up in case studies, organizational research, and the general press—for not having a conductor.[1] It does have a managing director, currently Ronnie Bauch, whom I met at a conference on national intelligence organizations a few years ago. When Ronnie has been generous enough to speak to students at Stanford Business School, I delight in introducing him as "the leader of a leaderless organization."

Bauch immediately corrects me, of course. Orpheus, he explains, is not "leaderless" at all. Instead, it is a "multileader" organization where leadership tasks are shared and rotate among the members. For instance, not only is there no conductor, other key positions such as first violinist also rotate. As one article notes, "A different core group shapes each piece and then works with the whole ensemble."[2] The advantage of this sort of organization, rare though it may be, can best be understood by considering what happens under the traditional, strong-leader organization—in classical music, organizations that are "conductor-centric." In such systems, everyone orients to the conductor. They focus on his (it is typically a "he") pronouncements and stop paying as much attention to each other—all eyes are on the front, as it were, or in a typical company, focused on the top. People look to that leader to provide direction and to take responsibility for solving and even identifying problems. Moreover, under a strong leader whose opinions become what the organization does, members soon learn to quell their own voices. Why bother advocating a point of view or providing information or assistance unless asked, because it will be ignored in any event? As Eric Bartlett, a cellist with both Orpheus and the New York Philharmonic, has stated, "If even a great conductor is empowered to make all the important decisions musicians start to play in a more passive way."[3]

When creative, independent people don't get much say in what their organization does, job dissatisfaction and disengagement are high: "When Harvard Business School professor J. Richard Hackman studied job attitudes among people working in 13 different job groups, he discovered that symphony orchestra musicians ranked below prison guards in job satisfaction . . . when asked about their satisfaction with opportunities for career growth, symphony orchestra musicians fared even worse, ranking 9th out of 13 surveyed job categories."[4]

In an ensemble that never gets larger than 40 people, such responses are a problem, but in large companies, they can prove particularly harmful. Economists talk about the problem of "free-riding"—people coasting on the efforts of others and not contributing as much as they could to the common good. Economic theory argues that this problem is likely to be particularly acute in large organizations. After all, if you are just one of many thousands, why should you take individual responsibility and make some sustained effort to improve the situation, as your chance of making a substantial difference is going to be small—and this is particularly the case in leader-centric types of places. Moreover, your lack of effort is less likely to be noticed the larger the group. What a contrast with Orpheus. In the absence of a strong leader—in this case, a conductor—musicians have to collectively do for themselves what is left to the conductor to do in most other places. So, musicians take responsibility for fund-raising (Orpheus, like other classical music organizations, needs to supplement its income from recordings and performances with private donations). They take responsibility for constructing the programs the group will perform. As Bauch explained to me, musicians are not taught how to organize a program—a task typically done by the conductor. But a program has to have a beginning and an end, maybe an intermission, the music must be selected, and the order of performance decided. Without a conductor, the musicians take on these decisions themselves. Musicians also become responsible for managing the group's public relations activities, and it is the musicians, not the conductor that they don't have, that wind up taking collective responsibility for hiring new members of the ensemble when such replacements are necessary.

Four things happen because people are more responsible for the collective output of the organization and perform more diverse tasks. First of all, one of the best ways to learn something is by doing it—and being involved in public relations, programming, fund-raising, and hiring causes the members of Orpheus to develop competencies that they might not otherwise possess. Orpheus is only a part-time commitment for most of its members. Bauch notes that in their other lives, many of the group's members are professors in music programs or conductors of other orchestras. He claims that their experience in Orpheus has helped its members build the knowledge and skills—including leadership skills—that have made them so effective and sought after in these other roles.

One of the skills Orpheus members develop is the ability to listen to each other. In conductor-centric orchestras, musicians focus only or primarily on the conductor. Orpheus's musicians, by contrast, must learn to coordinate their playing with each other, and to do so, they must become better listeners. This collective mind and spirit comes through to make the music better. As the *Boston Globe*'s Richard Dyer has written, there is a "liberating intensity with which these musicians listen to one another."[5]

Second, without some strong central figure to whom to defer, members invariably not only do more things but initiate and own their actions. Orpheus is not an organization where people say, "It's not my job" or wait to be told what to do. In a world in which many organizations struggle to get people to take responsibility and feel personally involved in their employer's success or failure, Orpheus does not face that problem at all. That's because the best way to have people *feel* engaged and responsible is to give them decisions to make and to actually have them *be* responsible—precisely what occurs when there is no dominant leader to look to for all the answers.

Third, people use more of their gifts, skills, and energy in the interests of Orpheus because they are fully engaged. Bauch strongly believes that most people bring only about 20 percent of their talent and energy to their jobs. They do what they are told or permitted to do and soon learn to leave much of their potential outside. You can see this clearly in the airline industry; many pilots and flight attendants have advanced degrees, and some even run successful businesses in their free time. But because they are not asked for their input—and in fact, because in most airlines they are told in many subtle and not-so-subtle ways that their opinions are not valued—they soon learn to withhold their insights and just do what they are told. This is not the case in Orpheus. With decision-making responsibility in their own hands, people are more fully committed to the organization's success and therefore devote more of their energy and attention to the chamber orchestra.

And fourth, in taking more responsibility, doing more jobs, and sharing decision-making duties, members learn how to speak up, communicate their ideas more effectively, and deal with the rejection when, in a given instance, they don't get their way. As Bauch has noted, "Students are never encouraged to speak up during normal orchestra rehearsals . . . We want to help them find their own voice, give them confidence that what they have to say is important. They need to know to express themselves, and have to deal with having their ideas rejected."[6]

Of course, there are costs to the member-centric organizational structure of Orpheus. The orchestra spends more time rehearsing, because without a conductor to make all the decisions, musicians must decide among themselves precisely how they want to play a piece. Auditioning new members takes extra time, since candidates are evaluated by more people and also must be assessed not only on their musical prowess but also on their ability to fit with the group's collaborative, egalitarian culture. And in a world that expects hierarchy, there's always pressure for Bauch and his colleagues to justify and defend their nonhierarchical way of operating. Bauch points out that this is a problem even with Orpheus's own board. Thus one of his goals as managing director has been to get the entire organization and its operations—not just the part that involves the musicians—to embrace the multileader, distributed-power model.

People immediately dismiss the Orpheus model as not having much relevance for more traditional business organizations. "These are musicians," is a comment I have often heard. But the problems with leader-centric organizations noted above are endemic in the corporate world—employees feeling disengaged, feeling not responsible, not speaking up, not learning a broad set of skills, and, most of all, abdicating attempts to remedy problems when they are noticed. Even "activists" limit their actions: consider the now-famous Sherron Watkins, who blew the whistle on Enron's pervasive accounting problems and corporate fraud. She wrote an internal memo to then-CEO Ken Lay, but when he chose to dismiss her concerns, she didn't do anything else to remedy or bring to light the financial improprieties she had observed.

The advantages of listening to more people and using this collective intelligence are many. The book *The Wisdom of Crowds* lays out the case for the better predictions and forecasts that emerge from markets and other structures that aggregate the insights and intelligence of multiple individuals, even when those individuals are not themselves experts.[7] For example, Google, rather than assigning all responsibility for new products to one person, allows any employee to post ideas on an internal Web site. Colleagues then vote for the ideas they like, so popular projects rise to the top and receive strategic attention. This idea—which essentially takes advantage of the collective intelligence of the group—is spreading to other companies as well.

But it's not just aggregating predictions or opinions—elements of multileader organizations—that are spreading to traditional businesses. The idea of self-managed teams and the advantages of teams—their ability to get people involved and also to develop the skills of team members—have long been recognized in the management literature.[8] The problem is that for the talents and ideas of others to emerge, leaders need to step back and provide the space for this to occur. Some companies—Patagonia, the outdoor clothing and equipment company, and Sun Hydraulics, the hydraulic cartridge valve and manifold company, are a couple that come to mind—have been built with cultures that emphasize more distributed leadership. But these are rare examples. As Rakesh Khurana has described, the business press, corporate boards of directors, and social expectations have conspired to have companies search for corporate saviors in the form of strong leaders.[9] And few who reach leadership positions have the modesty to let others share the limelight.

It is deliciously ironic. Even as companies bemoan the lack of leadership talent and spend large sums of money on leadership development programs, executive education, and workshops, their very leader-centric structures and cultures hinder these leadership development initiatives. As Morgan McCall, among others, pointed out long ago, the best way to foster leadership and develop leaders is to treat people like leaders and give them leadership responsibility.[10] And what better way to do that than to build organizations like Orpheus, where everyone feels—and is—in charge? It may seem counterintuitive, but by not appointing one leader for every new problem and initiative, you might actually help your people make beautiful music together.

Part II

Creating Effective Workplaces

CHAPTER 7

Stop Picking Employees' Pockets

It Seldom Fixes Anything

WHEN LARGE COMPANIES fall into financial difficulties, it always amazes me to see where they turn first for help in overcoming their problems—to their hourly workers and other frontline employees, who are asked to take pay cuts and reductions in benefits such as health insurance and pensions. In 2005, General Motors asked the United Auto Workers union to reopen their contract prior to its expiration in 2007 so the company could reduce health insurance benefits for current and retired employees. After enduring a four-month strike by Southern California grocery workers, Albertsons, Kroger, and Safeway ultimately managed to freeze the pay scales of existing employees, hire new people at lower wages, and raise health-insurance copayments, all in an effort to meet Wal-Mart's low-cost challenge in the grocery business.

But it is perhaps in the airline industry where asking employees to reduce their wages has been most pronounced. Since 2001, US Airways, American, Delta, Northwest, and United have all dug into their employees' pockets, often many times, in an effort to lower costs and survive in an extremely competitive environment. In the fall of 2004, for instance, US Airways reduced the pay rate for reservation agents by another 21 percent, taking the pay of Kelly Orr down to $13 an hour from the $25 she once made. The airline also cut the pay of flight attendants by an additional 21 percent, taking the pay of Randy Brooks from the high $40,000 range to the low $30,000 level.[1] Pilots have suffered similar sorts of reductions at most of the major carriers.

But in case you haven't noticed, in spite of the many rounds of wage cuts, the major airlines have continued to lose market share to the discount carriers such as JetBlue and Southwest and have continued to bleed money. Grocery chains have also continued to lose customers to Wal-Mart and Costco on the one hand and to Whole Foods Market on the other, and still face margin pressures and profit problems. That's because the solution management seized on—cutting workers' pay—actually doesn't do very much to make organizations more profitable and competitive or even, in some cases, to reduce costs. Instead, cutting employee wages often worsens company problems. Hourly rates of pay simply don't do nearly as much as most people seem to believe to determine a company's—or even a country's—competitive advantage. That's because wage rates are not the same thing as labor costs, labor costs don't equal total costs, and—in many instances—while it is nice to be low cost, low costs and profits aren't perfectly correlated either.

Consider first some surprising facts about the effects of wage rates on the competitiveness of nations. Japan runs a trade *surplus* with China, even though Japan has higher wages. High-wage, presumably high-cost, countries such as Canada and Germany also run trade surpluses. You might assume that Italy—another high-wage country and a major manufacturer of clothes and shoes—would have a difficult time competing in a global market where apparel and footwear are typically made in low-wage locations.

For example, Levi Strauss has closed all of its U.S. plants, and Nike continually fends off critics of worker conditions in the Asian factories where its shoes get made. But Italy, too, boasted a trade surplus, even in shoes, until quite recently. Meanwhile, the United States runs a trade *deficit* of about $600 billion, even though it has lost its position in the list of high-wage countries. U.S. average employee wages are actually 40 percent below those in the United Kingdom, 38 percent below Japan, 23 percent below the average for Western Europe, and even below the average wage in Ireland.[2]

What's true for countries is also true for companies. The competitive success of airlines such as Southwest, Alaska, and Jet-Blue depends on lots of things besides wage rates. For a start, it's nice to be able to offer customers a product or service offering they actually want to buy. In the airline industry, three of the four U.S. airlines rated the best in terms of the customer experience in 2004 were the so-called low-cost airlines; the only nondiscounter in the top four was Alaska. According to a study that examined the customer service experience—on-time performance, number of customer complaints, denied boardings, and mishandled baggage—there was a performance gap between the legacy carriers and the low-cost carriers, which, although they are supposedly no-frills, actually outperformed their rivals.[3] Virgin Atlantic Airways has consistently pursued a strategy of offering more amenities and better service for both its business-class and economy fares, and has generated a profit when other airlines have struggled. After further upgrading its business-class seats and service in 2004, the carrier reported a 26 percent increase in business-class traffic for the fiscal year ending in February 2005.[4] And Singapore Airlines has been one of the most consistently profitable air carriers over the past several decades, in large measure because of its reputation for outstanding customer service. Furthermore, both Singapore and Virgin are able to charge more for trips covering the same routes as competitors, belying the idea that airline service is a commodity and people won't pay more to get more.

In the automobile industry as well, profits depend on more than just costs. Profits also are affected by brand image and product design and quality, all of which affect how much people are willing to pay for a car. While General Motors whines about its cost disadvantage because of its health care expenditures and high, unionized wage rates, Toyota achieved almost $6,000 per vehicle more in *net revenue* in 2004, according to the 2005 Harbour Report. Toyota was able to get its customers to pay more for each car because it did not have to offer as many rebates, price concessions, and financing discounts to get customers to purchase its vehicles.[5]

And even forgetting about the revenue part of the picture and focusing only on costs doesn't change the conclusion that labor rates are overrated as a source of competitive advantage or disadvantage, because labor *rates* are only imperfectly associated with labor *costs*. In 2004, it took Ford Motor Company on average almost one-third more labor hours to manufacture a car than it did Toyota.[6] So Ford begins with a cost disadvantage even if its rate of pay is the same.

In the summer of 2004, it cost US Airways 11.18 cents to fly one seat one mile, while it cost United 9.83 cents, Alaska 10.63 cents, and Frontier and Southwest, both discount carriers, only 8.09 cents.[7] But in the spring of 2004 the captain of an Airbus A320 or a Boeing 737 with ten years of seniority made an hourly rate of $194 at Alaska, $175 at Southwest, $151 at Frontier, but only $143 at United and $149 at US Airways.[8] Yes, Southwest paid its pilots—and its first officers and pilots with different levels of seniority—over 20 percent *more* than United, even before additional rounds of wage givebacks further increased the wage premium. Southwest also paid more than US Airways, even as that carrier floundered in bankruptcy and feared Southwest's entry into its Philadelphia hub market.

It also turns out that *total* costs depend on more than just *labor* costs. An analysis of the cost of flying from Washington, DC, to South Florida in 2004—the same route, using the *identical* equipment—revealed that United's fuel consumption costs were 60 percent higher and its maintenance costs were more than 30 percent higher than JetBlue's.[9] Similarly, a former United Airlines pilot now working for JetBlue told me that Airbus, the manufacturer of the A319 and A320, had noted that different airlines flying the identical plane identical distances in identical weather had different fuel utilization. JetBlue was, according to Airbus, significantly more efficient than other airlines. In the fall of 2004, the company challenged its pilots to cut fuel consumption 1 percent, thereby saving $3 million per year. The pilots actually cut fuel use by 3 percent, and JetBlue's fourth quarter 2004 profit was the equivalent to the amount of fuel savings it had achieved.

The problem is that a fixation on labor costs diverts management's attention from other aspects of operations that might provide even more leverage. Take another example: in contract manufacturing, companies such as Solectron will tell you that labor costs constitute at most 25 percent of total costs, while materials and other costs constitute the rest—and this in an industry with little R&D and marketing.

Not only do labor costs not equate to total costs, even labor costs themselves depend on two things: the rate of pay—the thing that seems to draw the most management attention—and employee productivity of the people—what people actually accomplish on the job. Unfortunately, wage givebacks often alienate employees and reduce their willingness to provide discretionary effort and ideas that can enhance productivity and performance. Paying less also leads to turnover among the existing workforce—and turnover costs money—as well as a competitive disadvantage in the labor market where companies must try to attract the best and the brightest and the most motivated people.

Pilots, to continue with the airline example, can alter costs and revenues dramatically depending on their decisions and effort. According to the JetBlue pilot mentioned above, a highly motivated pilot, someone with experience and skill, can constantly seek shortcuts and more favorable altitudes from air traffic control, can use fuel-saving techniques such as taxiing with one engine and planning more efficient climbs and descents, and can help other crew members to get the plane turned around, thereby enhancing on-time performance. A less skilled or experienced pilot may not know all these ways to increase efficiency. An unmotivated or angry pilot can "work to rule"—no shortcuts; no extra customer service; no putting in voluntary overtime to avoid canceled flights (with their attendant costs) caused by pilot shortages; no trying to save fuel; and as a result, no savings and much higher costs. The pilot slowdown at United during the summer of 2000 forced hundreds of flight cancellations and delays, alienated customers, and cost the airline millions.

It is difficult to have motivated, committed, and engaged employees when those employees feel as if they have been abused and mistreated, asked for sacrifices not shared by others, and forced to pay for the strategic mistakes of senior management. When companies are facing their greatest competitive challenges is precisely the time when they most need employee loyalty and effort. That's why John Whitney, when he took over a near-bankrupt Pathmark Supermarkets in 1972, actually *raised* the salaries of store managers. As he told me, the last thing you want during a turnaround is to have your best people heading for the door, worrying about their futures, or not putting forth their best efforts. More recently, when child-care provider Childtime Learning Centers faced financial stringency, instead of making cutbacks, it invested in training and development, particularly for its center managers, and in recruiting better people who would stay with the company longer. Instead of getting into the typical death spiral in which expense cuts hurt productivity and then the company winds up cutting even more, Childtime was able to build value through its investments in its people and was eventually purchased by an Australian firm.[10]

Instead of blaming employee salaries for the consequence of every strategic error and management miscue, leaders would be well served to look at the usual suspects—quality and service—and focus on fixing those proven ingredients for success. These fixes most often require the efforts of the front-line people, and you don't want to alienate them by picking their pockets. But most importantly, companies should at least get the facts about the real sources of their poor performance, and avoid the sloppy thinking that equates labor rates with labor costs, labor costs with total costs, and total costs with profits and success. Faulty assumptions lead to bad decisions, which invariably produce lousy business results. You don't have to look further than the U.S. airline and automobile industries to see the truth of that statement.

CHAPTER 8

Let Workers Work

The Downsides of Having People
Manage Their Own Benefits

FACING GROWING COMPETITION and financial pressure, many companies have responded by cutting employee benefits to maintain their profits. A 2005 survey by Deloitte found that 90 percent of the responding companies planned to rein in costs during 2006 by changing their active employees' health plans.[1] Companies are also cutting back pension benefits, either freezing or canceling defined benefit plans—those programs that pay retired employees a fixed sum depending on their final wage and years of service—and either eliminating retirement programs completely or substituting defined contribution plans where employees manage their own accounts and assume more of the risk of ensuring they have the financial resources to permit them to retire.

So, a 2004 Deloitte survey discovered that only 10 percent of corporate executives would offer a traditional defined benefit retirement plan if they were able to create their companies' retirement benefit programs from scratch.[2] Many people predict a similar movement in health care plans, with programs migrating from defined benefit to defined contribution plans. In these types of plans, employers put up some money and employees are then largely responsible for using that money to purchase insurance and manage their own health care. The advantage to employers is that their financial obligations are known—they are determined by the money to be allocated to the plans—and more controllable. In each of these changes in both pensions and health care, the trend is clear—companies are shifting risk and liability, and also decision-making responsibility, to their employees; indeed, such a shift is an explicit objective of many of these changes.

But companies, in their haste to cut short term, visible costs and transfer decision making to their workforce, haven't thought very carefully about the implications of these actions for their profitability and productivity. If they did, they would see that many of the changes will have feedback effects that can either limit or even eliminate the supposed benefits. For one thing, such changes ignore the time and expertise required to manage benefits. Moreover, the emphasis on employee responsibility for their own benefits management (1) ignores the advantages of specialization and the division of labor, (2) causes employees to spend time on issues that are far removed from their primary jobs, diverting effort from their work, and (3) removes an important way in which companies have traditionally competed to attract talent, at the very moment that talent is going to become increasingly scarce.

The move toward giving employees responsibility for benefits is striking and huge. Many companies are experimenting with insurance plans that make their people more "cost conscious" by taking an active role in health care decision making. For example, Definity Health, now part of United Healthcare, and one of the vendors of consumer-driven insurance programs, boasts on its Web site that "you, the consumer of health care services, are given direct access to your health care dollars and the freedom to make choices."[3] The shift to defined contribution retirement plans, already well under way, does the same thing for retirement—people are responsible for deciding whether or not to participate in an employer's program, how much to contribute, and where and how to invest their retirement assets. There are three big problems with these changes in who makes the decisions. First of all, remember Adam Smith and the famous pin-manufacturing factory, which illustrated the efficiency gains from specialization and a division of labor? The whole premise of specialization is that people who only have to learn about a subset of decisions and activities can become more expert than those who have to cover a broader range of issues. Specialization permits people to delve more deeply into a subject. And specialization gives people practice and experience and the proficiency that comes from that practice and experience. In other words, specialization promotes efficiency. Michael Jordan may have been a great professional basketball player, but his career as a baseball player was short and undistinguished. In every field of endeavor, outstanding achievement and great performance come from years of experience and hours of practice.[4]

Making everyone—and I mean everyone, including people with limited education, limited resources, and possibly even limited reading and English language skills—responsible for managing their health care and retirement decisions violates the most basic ideas of specialization and expertise. It is important to recognize that decisions about health care and retirement are decisions with substantially more complexity, financial importance, and risk than the typical consumer purchase decisions so often used in the misguided analogies I see. Confronted with too many choices that they don't necessarily want to make, many employees literally don't do anything. There is convincing evidence, in the case of retirement benefits, that the more choices employees face, the less likely they are to sign up for *any* plan, thereby forgoing employer matching dollars. And the more investment options they have, the more likely they are to leave their assets in money market accounts that don't provide sufficient returns to ensure a decent prospect of retirement.[5]

Second, when do employers think people are going to make these benefits decisions and gain the expertise to do so? Clearly some of this learning and decision making will occur on the job. My employer, Stanford University, occasionally runs retirement seminars during the workday and provides calculators on its Web site to help people navigate the myriad choices and complexities of benefit management; and once a year we also have a series of benefits fairs that people can take time off to attend. This is all nice, and maybe even pleasurable for some—for example, a young Texans Credit Union employee remarked, "Co-pays, 401(k)s, flexible spending accounts—it was fun figuring out what everything meant."[6] But I wonder if anyone actually bothers to calculate how much time is diverted from people's principal work activities to the task of managing their benefits.

Of course, every action provokes a counteraction, and employers' decisions to force people to make time-consuming decisions that tax their abilities has stimulated the development of an industry to—surprise!—do for a fee do what companies themselves used to do for their workforce in simpler times. So, Health Advocate, a firm founded in 2001 by five former Aetna U.S. Healthcare employees, charges companies a monthly fee of $1.25 to $3.95 per employee to help people deal with their health insurance decisions.[7] Another company, inAssist, markets claims assistance to employers as an employee benefit, also charging a per-employee-per-month fee.[8] Medical claims assistance is a growing business because dealing with insurance companies and coverage can tax even the most skilled and educated workers. But how about this for an idea: instead of offering assistance and advice as an added benefit, or hoping that somehow employees can cope on their own and not spend too much company time doing so, why not offer benefits that don't require a PhD to figure out?

It is also important to note that much of the shifting of risk from companies to their employees is economically inefficient. That's because companies can spread risk—for instance, of incurring a catastrophic medical expense—across their entire employee base while individual employees have much more difficulty in diversifying their risk. Moreover, economists argue, for risk-diversification among other reasons, individual employees are going to be more risk averse than companies; in the case of medical insurance, for example, many employees are reluctant to retire or even change jobs for fear of losing health insurance. One survey found that more Americans were afraid of rising health care costs than terrorism or even losing their jobs.

If something like insurance is more valuable to an individual than it costs a company to provide, the obvious course is for the company to purchase that product or service and provide it to the employee—precisely the opposite of what is occurring. The current trend of off-loading of risk to employees is contrary to much of conventional economic theory, which argues for the assumption of risk by those entities—in this instance companies—that have a comparative advantage in doing so.

Finally, when companies shift decision-making tasks and risks onto their workforce, they make themselves less desirable as employers, compared with companies that offer more generous employee assistance. Here a little historical perspective helps us understand the likely consequences of such moves. Companies began offering benefits such as retirement and health care coverage in the early part of the twentieth century for several, quite self-interested, reasons. First of all, these efforts, sometimes referred to as "welfare capitalism," helped to forestall unionization drives. Second, companies offered these benefits to attract and retain employees. Ford Motor Company, for instance, experienced such high turnover that it could scarcely operate its assembly lines. Raising wages and providing employee assistance represented an effort to build a workforce that would provide competitive advantage. Similarly, Eastman Kodak's pension efforts arose from its enlightened self-interest in attracting an experienced, educated, and loyal labor force.[9]

There has been much commentary on the coming shortage of labor throughout the industrialized world, a consequence of declining birth rates. In the United States, the passing from the workforce of the baby-boom generation is expected to create numerous job openings and labor shortages in vital industries such as oil and gas, air traffic control, and government, as well as throughout the economy more generally. If there is one thing that is clear from looking at *Fortune*'s best places to work lists, it is that most of those companies offer benefits that are more generous than standard for their industry or for the economy as a whole. Thus, it seems ironic that companies are cutting one of the ways that they have traditionally attempted to achieve an advantage in attracting employees just at the moment that the competition for labor is about to increase.

Shifting decision making and the risk for funding retirement and health care, as well as other benefits, onto the workforce at first glance looks like a shrewd way to take costs out of the system. But many of these gains are ephemeral. Individual employees do not have a comparative advantage in decision making about retirement and certainly not about medical care, and the time required to manage their various accounts is often going to come out of time spent on other work. Moreover, worrying about retirement and health care can distract people's focus and make concentration and effort more difficult. Perhaps that's why the best employers offer more generous benefits and use the idea of specialization and comparative advantage to have decisions made by those most qualified to make them, in partnership with their people.

CHAPTER 9

Why Spy on Your Employees?

Building Trust in the Workplace

WITH THE EXPLOSION of communications technology have come two trends that seem at once inexorable and logically interrelated. The first is employees' growing use of company resources, particularly computers and Internet connections but also personal digital assistants, instant messaging, and telephones, for personal business or recreation while at work. ComScore Networks found that, excluding auctions, 59 percent of all 2001 Web purchases made in the United States were made from the workplace. A survey by Vault.com reported that 47 percent of employees spend at least a half hour a day cruising the Web for personal reasons. According to a study by IDC Research, 30 to 40 percent of employee Internet activity is for personal reasons, and SexTracker noted that about 70 percent of all Internet porn traffic occurs during workday hours—the obvious implication being that a lot of this activity is going on instead of work. A June 2000 Angus Reid Group study reported that 75 percent of those surveyed reported reading news or sports headlines at work, 67 percent reported doing comparison shopping, 55 percent reported sending or reading [personal] e-mail, 49 percent checked the stock market at work, 45 percent reported shopping online, and 22 percent reported playing games using the Internet while presumably on the job.[1]

The second trend constitutes what at first glance appears like a logical employer reaction to all this employee activity. Companies have installed myriad forms of software and equipment to monitor their people's Internet and telephone use. And they then use the results of that monitoring to take action. For instance, a 2004 American Management Association survey found that 60 percent of employers used software to monitor incoming and outgoing e-mail and one-quarter had terminated an employee for violating e-mail policy. A 2005 survey conducted by AMA and the ePolicy Institute reported that 76 percent of employers monitored their employees' Web site connections, 65 percent used software to block connections to some Web sites, and 26 percent had fired workers for misusing the Internet. Employers frequently tell employees that their computer and e-mail use are being monitored, with more than 80 percent informing their workers that the company is monitoring content, keystrokes, and time spent at the keyboard. And most employers have established policies governing personal e-mail use (84 percent) and personal use of the Internet (81 percent).[2] Employers also manage telephone use: some 57 percent block access to 900 lines, 51 percent monitor the amount of time employees spend on the phone and the specific numbers called, and 19 percent tape the calls of employees who work in some specific job categories.

Such actions seem sensible on the surface. After all, there's a lot at stake. A 2004 AMA survey found that 10 percent of the respondents reported spending more than half the workday— four hours or more—on e-mail, and some 86 percent acknowledged engaging in personal e-mail correspondence while at work. Furthermore, companies are worried about the legal liability of having inappropriate material displayed on computer screens or illegally downloaded copyrighted material in their systems. About one in five employers in the AMA survey reported being ordered by either a court or a regulatory authority to produce employee e-mail as part of some proceeding, and some 13 percent said they had to fight claims of harassment or discrimination based on employee e-mail content.

But like many management decisions concerning employees, things aren't as clear-cut as they might appear at first when we consider the real long-term consequences. Maybe it actually makes sense to let people do personal business while at work, or even spend some time goofing off. And maybe spying on your employees and trying to control their Internet and telecommunications activities isn't such a great idea after all.

Let's pretend companies got their most desired wish—people stopped doing any personal business such as online banking and stock trading at work. What might happen? Many households now have two working parents and, given the stagnation in average wages in the United States, more and more people work more than one job. So, if more people are working more hours at more jobs, and they can't do personal business at work, then there is a logical consequence: there will be more absenteeism as people have to take time off from work to attend to personal issues. According to a national survey conducted in the United Kingdom by the Chartered Institute of Personnel and Development, the average employee takes 8.5 sick days a year, and about one-third of their employers believe that more than 20 percent of this absence is not genuine. Estimates are that employee absence costs the United Kingdom economy more than $20 billion a year.[3] In the United States, in 2003 the cost of unscheduled absences was estimated as $800 per employee per year, with the leading cause of absenteeism being family-related issues.[4] If people can't do any of their personal business while at work, they simply won't be at work as often.

Second, people don't like being electronically monitored, although they may be getting used to it. So, ironically, even as companies talk about the importance of employee engagement and building a more committed and motivated workforce, they may be doing things—and spying on their people is certainly one such thing—that can make employee attitudes worse. Computer monitoring is often perceived as stressful, and research shows that people are less satisfied with both the task they are doing and with their supervisor when they are being watched.[5] Another study found that task performance was lower for monitored people, unless they had some control over the monitoring.[6]

Third, when you constrain what people can do and limit their freedom, you set in motion a process called psychological reactance.[7] As one simple example, have you ever noticed that you most need and want to get up and move around the airplane to go to the bathroom or stretch your legs right after the "Fasten Seat Belt" light comes on? People rebel against perceived constraints. And this resistance is also consistent with the psychological principle of scarcity—that people want more of what they are told they can't have.[8] Telling people they can't use the Internet or send personal e-mail therefore increases these activities' desirability. So, in many instances, companies have inadvertently turned somewhat boring and routine work—people's primary jobs—into an interesting intellectual challenge: can they manage to find some way to outsmart the various security systems that limit their freedom?

Fourth, companies need to beware of self-fulfilling prophecies—people responding to expectations for their behavior by doing things that make those expectations come true. One reason why the self-fulfilling prophecy operates is because people self-label and desire to behave in ways consistent with how they see themselves. For example, if people are labeled as smart, they will not only try to live up to this high expectation, they will also see themselves as more intelligent and be motivated to act in ways consistent with this self-conception. Conversely, if people are implicitly labeled as untrustworthy and dishonest—the logical implication of being monitored and told what to do—they can respond to that label by behaving in a less trustworthy and honest fashion, but one that is consistent with the expectations communicated for who they are and how they act.

Fifth, surveillance regimes can encourage those in authority to try and entrap the people being watched, making it more likely that companies will actually incite bad behavior and therefore, that proscribed actions will take place. Such entrapment acts as a way of justifying the need for surveillance in the first place. In a series of experiments, when the person doing the surveillance was more involved in and committed to the monitoring activity, that individual was more likely to engage in behavior that actually encouraged the person under surveillance (actually an assistant helping with the experiment) to cheat. Participants who felt negatively toward the person they watched—a logical consequence of that person being labeled as untrustworthy—were also more likely to engage in entrapment activities. As the study noted, understanding the consequences of surveillance and penalties for violating rules requires assessing the impact on those enforcing the rules as well as those subject to them.[9]

And there is a sixth consequence of electronic surveillance and proscribing what people can do with their time on the job, and this may be the most important consequence of all: monitoring your employees makes it very hard to create a climate of trust. In a classic experimental demonstration of the connection between surveillance and trust, participants were given two subordinates—actually confederates of the experimenter—to supervise while the experimenter was ostensibly away doing an errand. Although the two confederates performed objectively identically and behaved similarly, they were *not* under identical surveillance—one was randomly assigned to be closer and more visible to the subject than the other and, in other variants of the paradigm, the subject was requested to check up on one "subordinate" more than the other. The results show that the amount of surveillance someone engages in affects the climate of trust or distrust produced: people in a supervisory role reported placing less trust in those whom they supervised more closely.[10] And it is also likely that those being supervised will feel that they are not trusted—if they were, why would they be watched? All of these reasons explain why companies that actually achieve competitive advantage through their people management don't overcontrol or monitor how their employees spend their time. Jim Goodnight, cofounder and CEO of the highly successful software company SAS, facetiously told me in an interview that he considered giving people the Web addresses of sports and pornography sites so they wouldn't have to spend so much time finding them. Putting aside issues of creating a hostile work environment, Goodnight was quite clear that employees were responsible for doing their work in an effective and creative fashion, and how they spent their time and what they did with their computers at work was pretty much up to them. So, other than flagging for porn sites, SAS does not monitor its employee's Web use; it just tells its people to use company resources responsibly.

The basic prescription is simple. Before you implement the latest technology to monitor your workers, ask yourself what your decision says about how you think about your people. If you don't trust your employees, maybe you should get different ones. If you do trust them, or hope to build trust, treat them accordingly.

CHAPTER 10

All Work, No Play?

Maybe Long Hours Don't Pay

VISITING EUROPE IS FREQUENTLY not only pleasant but instructive. In Denmark, by about 5:15 on weeknights, the roads and sidewalks are crowded with people going home from work; and few people work on the weekends. In Spain, I visited San Sebastian to give a talk on ethics and had lunch with a group of executives from some of the region's top companies. In a dining room at the University of Navarra, we chatted through three courses and some bottles of excellent wine—the proverbial Spanish lunch. Visiting IESE, the business school headquartered in Barcelona, I learned that Spain takes its vacations seriously. The whole country essentially shuts down in August. In fact, during that month even the courts are closed except for emergency matters. Meanwhile, in France, there has been labor unrest over attempts to lengthen the 35-hour workweek; there is similar resistance to expanding working hours in Germany, as well. And in the United States? About one-quarter of all U.S. private-sector employees don't get any vacation at all, a 2006 Conference Board survey found that 40 percent of consumers had no plans to take a vacation in the next six months, and a Gallup survey revealed that 43 percent had no summer vacation plans.[1]

Ah, you must be thinking. Just what one might expect out of a continent, Europe, where people "work to live" rather than "live to work," where quality of life is important and leisure and family are central, and where, of course, as a consequence of this lifestyle, business isn't very productive and soon change will be thrust upon those self-indulgent Europeans.

But of course, this conventional wisdom is mostly wrong, as it is about many things. As an article in the *Economist* noted, by most measures European companies and economies are equal or approximately equal to the United States in terms of productivity and productivity growth. For instance, GDP per person grew 2.1 percent in America and 1.8 percent in Europe in the ten years prior to 2003, with the entire amount of even that small difference attributable to the underperformance of one country, Germany.[2] Leave out Germany, and job growth has been the same in the United States and Europe. Meanwhile, Europeans have chosen to take some of their wealth in leisure, while the United States has made a different choice. According to the *Economist*, "by one estimate the average American worker clocks up to 40 percent more hours during his life time than the average person in Germany, France, or Italy."[3]

There is little doubt that in working hours, as in many other aspects of work arrangements, the United States is different. According to a 2003 study published by the International Labour Office, the annual average duration of work in hours is higher in the United States than in any other of 18 industrialized countries except Japan.[4] Companies often make long hours sort of a loyalty test. In 2001, Neal Patterson, the CEO of Cerner, a software company headquartered in Kansas City, sent an e-mail to employees warning that their cars were too seldom in the parking lot before 8 a.m. or after 5 p.m.[5] Employees are expected to put their work and their employer first, and one way of demonstrating their commitment is by forgoing leisure and family. With cell phones and pagers and e-mail at home, work even intrudes on supposedly free time. The United States has, indeed, become a nation of workaholics. But is this sensible, even taking the relatively narrow perspective of what's best for companies and the economy and forgetting about the plight of the workers?

The simple equation of *hours worked* = *work output* may have made sense in the past when work was mostly agricultural labor and factory work. It is hard to plow more of a field without spending more time doing it, labor-saving machinery aside; and similarly, the longer a production line runs, the more it produces. Of course, the equation of working hours with output is less sensible when the content of work has shifted to innovation and creative content to a greater degree, but old habits and old ways of thinking die hard.

Furthermore, the long hours people work can have many costs that need to be taken into account when a company considers if working more hours really pays off. First of all, there is evidence that long work hours can have negative effects on mental health, can produce stress, and are associated with increased incidence of cardiovascular disease.[6] The stress caused by excessive work can, in turn, produce other behavioral problems with negative consequences, including smoking, alcoholism, and poor diet. Causality is obviously too complex and multifaceted to be easily and unambiguously assessed, but it is interesting that the United States, for all its great technology and spending on health care, does *not* have particularly good comparative health outcomes in terms of life expectancy. Although the United States ranks first in per capita health expenditures, according to a 2000 report by the World Health Organization, the country ranked only 24th in terms of life expectancy.[7] Maybe the long hours and curtailed time with family and friends is one of the reasons U.S. health care costs, including employer health care costs, are soaring.

Second, working long hours invariably leads to diminished concentration and focus and, as a consequence, to mistakes and accidents. That's why airline pilots, truck drivers, and—after a tragedy in a New York City hospital—medical interns have regulated working hours. As the quality movement teaches us, mistakes are much less costly to prevent than to discover and correct. This is particularly true for complex products such as software. SAS Institute is justly famous for its 35-hour workweek. But it is also famous for its high quality of customer service and programs that actually run as they are supposed to. CEO Jim Goodnight told me that because the company does not have people doing programming while they are exhausted, its programs have fewer bugs and therefore need less time and fewer people to find and correct programming mistakes. In fact, he claimed that the company had about one-third the number of "checkers" as Microsoft on a per-employee basis, even though the SAS system relies on an enormously complex and large body of code.

Third, companies face a coming demographic crunch. A Deloitte study noted that by 2008, skills and experience will begin to disappear from the job market. "Four industries in particular will suffer a mass exodus of employees: health care, manufacturing, energy, and the public sector."[8] And even as the baby boomers retire in droves, the people now entering the labor force come with a different set of priorities and preferences than their parents and grandparents. In part because they have seen companies lay off people who have devoted their lives to those same companies—in other words, loyalty has not been repaid—and in part because of different values, there really are generational differences in attitudes toward work and the working environment. Younger workers want different things and aren't willing to make the same trade-offs between work and outside interests and pursuits. As one senior executive in a large financial services firm commented, "It's almost like insubordination."

Contrary to myth and much conventional wisdom, European companies can and do compete successfully in global product and service markets, even with vacation and workweek policies that put their U.S. competitors to shame. At $23 billion Airbus, which over the past several years has outsold its bigger U.S. rival

Boeing in commercial aircraft sales, almost everyone takes their allotted five weeks of vacation, including three or four weeks during July or August. Airbus's most critical knowledge workers—junior engineers—get and often take as much as nine weeks off a year. And almost no one in the company regularly works weekends. Although Airbus has recently had production difficulties with its latest generation of planes, many of the operational problems stem from its politically determined organizational structure, not from the productivity of its employees. Moreover, even with its current sales difficulties, the company remains a formidable competitor.

Similarly, Banco Bilbao, headquartered in Spain, is one of the largest banks in the world, having bought operations literally around the globe. It, too, has kept its vacation and workweek policies in spite of operating in a globally competitive industry. And don't forget Nokia, the Finnish company that has successfully trumped the competition in the cell phone and personal digital assistant market. It, too, apparently has been successful in spite of the "misfortune" of being headquartered in a country where leisure and family time are priorities and where summer vacations are both long and utilized.

In fact, as a former doctoral student once commented to me, it is quite possible that these European companies and countries are not successful, as many think, *in spite of* their short workweeks and long vacations, but instead *because of* these very practices. The logic is simple. First, just as high wages cause companies to substitute capital for labor and use labor as efficiently as possible, thereby driving labor productivity up, so long vacations and shorter workweeks almost force organizations to be more disciplined in their management practices and processes. Endless, useless meetings? Less likely where work hours are a scarce resource. Inefficient work practices? Same story—limited labor hours put a premium on organizing work to be as productive as possible. And instead of just competing on the basis of brute force—of spending lots of time trying to get things done—companies are forced to be smarter about *what* they choose to do as well as *how* they go about doing it.

Second, being relaxed and refreshed can make people more productive and creative. The accounting firm Pricewaterhouse-Coopers has taken to shutting down for ten days over Christmas and five days over the Fourth of July, and sending notices to employees who haven't been taking their vacations—all in an effort to get people to take some time off. Company leaders said they "started their nationwide shutdown because people were not getting their batteries recharged."[9]

So, perhaps it is not so surprising that many of the Scandinavian countries rank the highest on Richard Florida's index of creative work.[10] Their very labor practices force them to compete on design, innovation, and creativity, instead of just throwing human resources at their competitive problems.

The moral for U.S. companies is clear. SAS Institute, with its 35-hour workweek, may not be some quaint anomaly, but instead a model for the future. It's time for the U.S. companies that have made late nights and short weekends a test of loyalty to come to terms with the myth that long hours and no vacations are good for the bottom line. In a business world ever more reliant on creative work and intellectual capital, taking care of the people whom you expect to be the source of your success seems like a better strategy. And with the changing work values of the generations entering the labor force and the coming demographic crunch, companies may soon have no choice but to adapt. Those places that do so first and most successfully will almost certainly be in the best competitive position.

CHAPTER 11

Sins of Commission

*Be Careful What You Pay For,
You May Get It*

ON A SUNNY SUNDAY AFTERNOON, my wife Kathleen and I went to Putnam Toyota in Burlingame, California, to test-drive a Camry. When we told the salesperson that we were deciding between the Camry and a couple of other cars and would probably not make a purchase that afternoon, he sent us down to the block to the place where the Camrys were kept, essentially blowing us off so he could wait on the next customer. This man, like most car salespeople, was paid by commission—encouraged to "move metal" and given no reward for building dealer loyalty. He did, in other words, just what he was being paid to do—and that did not include wasting time on people who weren't going to immediately purchase a car. Needless to say, when we finally decided to buy a Camry, it wasn't from Putnam but instead from Toyota 101 in Redwood City, which doesn't pay its salespeople on commission and instead has tried to build a customer service culture and encourage dealer loyalty.

Or consider another example of an incentive system gone awry. A few years ago the city of Albuquerque, New Mexico, faced a problem with its garbage collection. The truck crews weren't completing their assigned routes on time, landing the city with a huge bill for overtime pay. Believing in the power of financial incentives, the city hit upon a plan: pay the drivers for eight hours regardless of how long it actually took them to complete their routes, figuring that this strategy would highly motivate the crews to finish their tasks quickly.

When I have used this example and asked audiences to guess what the drivers would do, most have no trouble coming up with what actually happened. First, drivers found they could finish faster if they didn't bother to pick up all the garbage on their routes. Unfortunately, however, people whose pickups were missed would call the city, which would then have to send a truck to pick up their garbage, not a very cost-effective process. Second, drivers could finish their routes more quickly if they sped. But speeding causes accidents, and the city soon found itself paying out more money in accident claims. And third, the garbage collection teams could cut some time if they didn't go to the dump to drop off their loads as frequently; but this decision led to them driving the trucks over the legal weight limit and receiving fines when they arrived at the dump. In 2002, 15 of the 24 drivers with the highest incentive pay brought overweight trucks to the landfill most often. All of these added expenses wound up costing the city dearly, according to a grand jury that looked into why Albuquerque's apparent solution to its garbage collection cost problem—instituting incentive pay—wound up being *more* rather than less expensive.[1]

It may seem odd for me to complain about the use of individual incentives and their harmful effects when individual incentive pay, including commissions for salespeople, is so very much in fashion these days. Hewitt Associates, the compensation and human resources consulting company, reported that in 1991, 51 percent of the companies participating in its salary survey offered at least one plan that tied pay to performance, a proportion that had increased to 77 percent by 2003.[2] Nor is this trend confined just to the United States: a 2003 Hewitt survey of 115 organizations in Canada found that 81 percent had some form of pay for performance, up from 43 percent in 1994.[3] Even in Europe, Korea, and Japan, where individual pay for performance was historically much less prevalent, there seems to be inexorable pressure to copy the United States' example and introduce more individual, performance-based incentives. So, for instance, executives from Hanwha, a large Korean conglomerate, described the pressures they felt to adopt more individual pay for performance. Researchers from Recruit, a Japanese human resources and publishing company, also told me about the growing belief that individual pay for performance should be adopted by Japanese companies, even as their own studies showed the problems with moving in this direction.

The big push for incentive pay stems from a belief that if employees were just compensated appropriately, virtually very organizational and management problem could be solved. Company stock price not providing a good enough return for shareholders? Tie CEO compensation more closely to company performance, including shareholder return. Kids not learning enough in school? Institute merit pay for teachers.[4] The government not providing good enough service to its citizens because the workforce has too much of a "civil service" mentality? Implement pay for performance in the federal government.[5]

Some people who question the extensive use of incentive pay point out that employees are motivated by factors other than money and that most surveys show that people rank money far down the list of reasons why they join or remain at companies. I believe, however, that the most fundamental problem with individual financial incentives is that they actually work *too* well. Financial incentives have powerful effects not simply because people are motivated by the opportunity to earn more money. People mostly want to do a good job and please their colleagues and leaders so they can feel good about themselves and their job performance. Incentives provide information about what behaviors the organization values and which, among the many sometimes conflicting priorities, the company most cares about. It's the old adage of "follow the money" played out as people try to discern what they ought to do in order to do a good job.

But that's a problem. Most companies have production processes and objectives that are way too complicated to be adequately captured in any incentive scheme. Consider the effects of incentive pay for teachers. The idea is to reward teachers who more effectively teach their students. But how are we to measure what students learn? The most common answer is their score on some standardized test. So teachers are being rewarded for improving their students' test scores. There are many ways to do this, but certainly the easiest is to give the students the test questions, the answers, or both, in advance. In fact, that's just what economist Steve Levitt found in his study of teacher cheating. The greater the incentive for improving student performance on tests, the more likely it was that there would be cheating.[6]

Or, to take another example, think about the use of stock options to reward executives for company performance. Seems sensible, until you realize that executives don't actually have to hold their stock and can choose when to exercise their options and reap the financial gains. So options essentially *do* reward executives for getting the stock price up—but possibly just for one brief moment of time. There are many ways to enhance the stock price, and certainly one way is to provide financial information that exceeds expectations for company performance, that is almost too good to be true. Turns out that's pretty much the behavior stock option grants encouraged. There is evidence that the higher the option grants to senior executives, the more likely it was that their companies would subsequently have to restate their financial statements.[7]

The typical response to these tales is to note that the plans were too simplistic and needed to incorporate more dimensions of performance. So, for instance, the city of Albuquerque should have specified not only that its drivers needed to finish their routes but also needed to pick up all the garbage, adhere to weight and speed limits, and so forth. But as soon as the incentive plan is complicated in this way, the next question becomes the weighting given to each of the components of performance— in this instance, picking up the garbage, adhering to the laws, finishing early. Plans quickly become complex. I can recall sitting in the office of Ko Nishimura, then CEO of contract manufacturer Solectron. Ko believed in pay for performance and also understood the complexity of Solectron's business. The solution? An incentive pay plan so complicated that Ko, a very smart man with advanced degrees, had to take the plan out of his drawer and refer to it as he explained it to me. Although the plan may have been able to capture the complexities of the business in its myriad details, its very complexity had cost it any possibility of guiding behavior. People don't walk around with pay plans in their pockets or complicated details memorized. Ironically, the very thing that is necessary for incentives to guide behavior—simplicity—is the same thing that defeats the effectiveness of such plans except in the simplest of business cases.

By the way, many of the leading compensation consulting companies fully realize the problems involved in implementing individual incentive schemes. They continue to implement such plans because, as one senior executive of a major firm told me, their clients demand it and if they didn't do it, a competitor would. Moreover, as this executive went on to say, since such plans invariably had problems, the company would get invited back in an effort to fix the problems with the original plan, thereby generating additional work and fees.

It is interesting to speculate as to why companies continue to rely so heavily on financial incentive schemes, given their well-documented problems. Part of the answer may be the "extrinsic incentives bias," the belief that others are motivated primarily by money even if people know that they, themselves, are not. Believing in the power of financial incentives, they come to rely too much on this tool of management.[8]

But I think an even more important reason may be that financial incentives are apparently easier to tinker with than other determinants of individual and organizational performance. I say "apparently" because as the foregoing examples make clear, financial incentives often have undesired and unanticipated consequences. Nonetheless, one can change a pay system or a set of financial rewards fairly quickly and easily. It is much harder to change organizational culture, people's mind-sets and beliefs, their knowledge and skills, and how effectively they work and communicate with each other. Thus, financial incentives offer the mirage of the quick fix—and contemporary management seems to be enamored of that idea. That's the case even though there can obviously be no sustainable competitive advantage from something that is easily observed and readily imitated—and there is almost nothing as readily observed and as easily copied as an organization's financial reward system.

So, leaders face a choice. They can do the hard work and uncover and fix the root cause of performance problems—something that the quality movement and W. Edwards Deming would recommend. Or they can tinker with financial rewards and hope that somehow they hit upon a magic formula that actually captures the organization's priorities reasonably well or that their employees will take the incentive system seriously enough, but not so seriously as to try and game the system.

In this last observation is perhaps the most important recommendation about how to avoid the sins of "commission." As George Zimmer, founder and CEO of the off-price tailored-clothing retailer Men's Wearhouse observed, you want incentives to be just large enough but not too large. In other words, you want rewards to be large enough to be noticed and you want to use them to provide an occasion for celebration and recognition, to let the group come together and share successes and enjoy each other's companionship. But you certainly don't want to make the incentives so large that they begin to drive and thereby distort behavior.[9] In Zimmer's wisdom, of course, is embedded a wonderful paradox—incentives shouldn't be used to drive behavior, but instead to provide recognition and to share the company's success with its employees.

There are, unfortunately, few shortcuts in leadership—and using financial incentives to fix companies isn't one of them. Companies that succeed in building high-performing cultures communicate relentlessly about what really matters and why. So, at DaVita, the kidney dialysis company, every meeting or event, including quarterly analyst conference calls, begins with a discussion of the various components and measures of patient care—the company's highest priority. Companies also must ensure that people understand their business model, and what produces business success and why. That entails sharing information and mostly investing a lot of resources in ensuring that people not only have information but that they also have the ability to use the information for making better business decisions. Again, DaVita shows what can be done. At DaVita University, the company spends more than $10 million a year educating people at all levels, but particularly its facility administrators and its senior leadership, on the company's values and culture—the DaVita Way of Managing—and also on how to understand the various reports, what its business and business model is, and how to be more effective in making good strategic and operational decisions.

So the message is, be careful what you wish for, because you might get it, and implement commissions or other financial incentives with caution. And if you're going to use financial incentives to guide behavior anyway, at least think about how someone who takes the incentive seriously might behave as a consequence. This anticipation will frequently successfully forecast just what people will do, so at least if you get what you pay for, you will be prepared for it.

CHAPTER 12

More Mr. Nice Guy

Why Cutting Benefits Is a Bad Idea

THE DAILY HEADLINES tell the tale: companies are abandoning pension and health care benefits for both active employees and retirees. Retiree health benefits are under siege—an estimated 40 percent of companies with more than 5,000 employees no longer offer retiree benefits at all, and many others are increasing the amounts that retirees have to pay to maintain coverage.[1] Companies are also eliminating or curtailing other benefits for retirees, such as life insurance.[2] And active employees are expected to pick up more of the tab for their health care costs.

Defined benefit retirement plans—those that pay a guaranteed, fixed amount, often based on years of service and the final wage earned—are particularly at risk because the liabilities for paying those benefits appear on companies' balance sheets. There were nearly 40,000 defined benefits plans in existence in 1999; by 2002 almost 20 percent of them were shut down—and this does not include plans frozen by employers.[3] An October 2003 survey of 1,000 employers offering defined benefit plans found that 20 percent of the respondents had either already frozen their plans or were contemplating doing so. Meanwhile, the number of *For-*

tune 1000 companies offering defined benefit plans fell from 660 in 2000 to 622 just three years later.[4] Employers are moving to cash balance plans and defined contribution plans, have ceased offering retirement plans period, and are taking aggressive steps to cut their benefits costs.

These actions, which show no signs of abating, raise a number of issues. From a public policy standpoint, there are concerns about whether or not companies should be able to off-load past promises made to employees onto the general public. When people do not have health insurance—and estimates are that there at least 45 million uninsured in the United States—health care providers such as emergency rooms and government agencies wind up picking up the tab because, at least to this point, we don't intentionally let people die in the street. Similarly, people without sufficient money to retire become a financial burden on public welfare agencies and government agencies that must provide care for the elderly.

And there are issues of simple fairness. You may wonder how this is all legal. After all, when I buy a house, I can't unilaterally decide later to stop or change my mortgage payments. That's because bank loans involve contracts detailing specific terms, payment schedules, obligations, and penalties. Deferred compensation in the form of retiree medical benefits or promises to pay a pension usually take the form of general promises that simply imply employers will continue current practices. Companies cannot take away compensation already earned or accrued, but many employers explicitly reserve the right to change the terms of their benefits practices in the future—and it's perfectly legal for them to do so, even though it may not seem quite fair.

There is also the concern about the competitiveness of U.S. companies. Since health care and retirement are more nationalized in most other industrialized countries—supported by the government through taxes—U.S. employers, who shoulder the burden more directly, face costs that companies in other countries don't. And because there is always the temptation to cut benefits, which is what is going on now, as a way of shedding costs to become more competitive, this leaves those companies still offering benefits at a competitive disadvantage. The dynamics almost certainly point to a tipping point at which time more and more organizations will jettison their benefits programs because they will be in such a small minority they won't want to or won't be able to assume the cost burdens of offering employees benefits that no one else does.

But putting aside questions of the morality of breaking promises implicitly made to induce employees to come to work for a company, and even putting aside issues of who should pay for retirement and health care—individual employers or the general public through taxes—there remains the question of whether any of this behavior actually even makes sense for the companies doing it. It's far from clear that it does.

First of all, there are feedback effects that I'm not sure companies are fully taking into account. The most prominent such effect with respect to retirement is this: if people are worried about losing their health insurance when they stop working, or if people do not have sufficient pension benefits to afford to retire, they won't. Recall that mandatory retirement, except in a relatively delimited set of instances, was abolished in the 1970s, so people can work as long as they want to. Companies may wind up with an older workforce and less turnover than they anticipated. As a consultant for PricewaterhouseCoopers noted: "One of the reasons why employers have retirement plans, which they don't talk a lot about, is that there may come a point where you need people to retire . . . There may come a time when an employer has an oversized workforce and part of that workforce may include a highly [legally] protected class of employees who cannot afford to retire, yet are no longer high performers."[5]

That prospect may explain the behavior of IBM. In 1999, IBM tried to move a number of employees, including middle-aged and older workers, to a cash balance plan. After angry protests from employees, IBM backed down and said that anyone 40 or older with at least 10 years of service could remain in the old pension plan, in the process more than doubling the number of employees given a choice between the old plan and the new cash balance plan.[6] The company wound up settling an age discrimination suit based on its pension changes for some $320 million. But then, without changing the basic design of its new plan, IBM began working to make its 401(k) defined contribution plan more generous and encouraging employees to enroll in the plan. This was not just corporate beneficence. As Jim Rich, the chief investment strategist at IBM Retirement Funds noted, "Since its employees tend to retire at 60, IBM wants to make sure that they can keep doing so."[7]

The feedback effects in the case of medical insurance are also frequently perverse. If companies make it more expensive for people to see doctors or buy medicines, they won't. But this choice can actually increase costs down the road. A Harvard study found that "when confronted with higher payments for expensive, brand-name prescription drugs, many people stop taking the medication entirely," in the process jeopardizing their health and increasing the long-term costs of neglecting appropriate medical treatment.[8]

And there is yet another feedback effect that companies may not like. Retirement benefits, both pensions and health insurance, are a form of deferred compensation. Labor economists tell us that deferred compensation is often an efficient arrangement for several reasons. First of all, postponing the compensation expense saves the time value of money. But even more importantly, deferred compensation can help tie employees to their employers, reducing turnover and its associated costs and ensuring that companies build more experienced and skilled workforces. When people come to understand that the promises that have been made can, and frequently are, broken, they will respond like the football player in the movie *Jerry Maguire*, and say:

"Show me the money." The ability of *any* company to offer any form of deferred compensation depends on the credibility of its promise to provide payment later, and that credibility is, in many respects, not simply dependent on what that specific company does but also on what others have done and the general climate of trust—or distrust—that creates.

In addition to the feedback effects just enumerated, breaking promises and cutting employee perquisites has bad effects on employee morale and trust. Distrust in the workplace is rampant. A survey by the Discovery Group found that 52 percent of employees don't believe information they receive from senior management.[9] A Towers Perrin survey reported that less than a third of employees were committed to their jobs, and 43 percent said they weren't content.[10] These attitudes have resulted in rising turnover, particularly in the presence of reasonably decent labor market conditions. So, between March 2004 and March 2006, voluntary turnover for executives more than doubled from 4.0 to 8.8 percent, sales force turnover increased from 8.4 to 15.9 percent, professional and technical turnover rose from 7.6 to 12.7 percent, and production employee turnover soared from 7.5 to 17.5 percent.[11]

What a company offers its people—and the spirit with which it makes those offers—is worth far more than any market-determined dollar figure. Employees learn quickly whether they can trust their employer and how that employer really feels about them. They figure it out not through the endless platitudes promulgated in HR literature, but by watching what the organization *does* and the trade-offs it makes.

How would your organization have handled this situation? Some years ago, managers at SAS, the largest privately owned software firm in the world, faced a tough decision. An employee had drowned during a weekend fishing trip, and his two children were enrolled in the company's high-quality and heavily subsidized day-care program. Because their mother did not work for SAS, the kids were now technically ineligible to continue in the program. SAS could have quietly and apologetically given the kids the heave-ho, either immediately or after a month or so. But instead, the company agreed to let the children attend for two more years, until they were old enough to enter kindergarten. Although this may not look like the most grandiose of gestures, it sent an important message to all SAS employees: the company will take care of you if tragedy strikes. Maybe that's why SAS turnover has always been so low, saving the company millions and enabling it to implement a strategy based on long-term relationships with its customers.

Maybe companies such as SAS and many others on the *Fortune* best places to work list aren't just being kind and generous by trying to maintain benefits and take care of people even as other organizations break promises and cut perks. Building companies based on mutual trust and commitment just might be a lot more efficient than the alternative of arm's-length deals with both parties doing just what is required, and nothing more.

CHAPTER 13

Resumes Don't Tell

*Pick People for What They Can Do,
Not What They May Have Done*

MANY COMPANIES, their senior executives, and even executive recruiters frequently use flawed techniques to find, screen, and hire leadership talent. Perhaps the biggest problem is the undue emphasis placed on the resume, that ubiquitous piece of paper that describes the candidate's educational background, job experience, responsibilities, and accomplishments. Even though companies do search Web sites, personal home pages, and other online sources such as posted blogs and video files to check up on applicants, it is important to recognize that these searches are mostly designed to find problems or pathologies, not to assess what people can do. For hiring, the resume is still critical, which is why there is still a decent market in resume-processing software. But there are two big problems with resumes: they're all too often inaccurate and, even when they don't distort the candidate's background, they're pretty useless as a guide for hiring.

Lying on resumes is apparently quite common. In early 2006, the resume-counseling service ResumeDoctor.com released the results of a study reporting major misstatements on 42.7 percent of the 1,000 resumes it examined. In an online survey conducted by the Society for Human Resource Management, more than 60 percent of the 373 human resource executives who participated reported finding inaccuracies on resumes.[1] There is even a Web site, www.fakeresume.com, that was established with the express purpose of helping people fabricate their credentials.[2] The editor of *Executive Recruiter News* estimated that between 5 and 15 percent of even senior executives had resumes that contained some form of fabrication or omission. A number of senior executives who faked aspects of their resumes have been uncovered. Here's a list from a *CFO* article: "Ken Lonchar, CFO of Veritas Software; Ronald Zarrella, chairman and CEO of Bausch and Lomb; Bryan J. Mitchell, chairman and CEO of MCG Capital; Ram Kumar, director of U.S. research for Institutional Shareholder Services; and Quincy Troupe, poet laureate of California."[3] Nor is this problem confined to the United States. The Institute of Management and Administration in the United Kingdom reported that lying on resumes is a trend that is growing worldwide, increasing 15 percent just between 2001 and 2002.[4]

People lie about the number of years they've worked at a particular job, they exaggerate their accomplishments, they sometimes make up educational credentials, and they often don't disclose the real reason they left a job.[5] And people who lie justify their behavior by noting that in today's dog-eat-dog world, all is fair in an effort to secure employment. The founder of the Web site that trains people in how to embellish their credentials argues that since most people do it, you have to as well, just to remain competitive in the job market. Companies' use of resume-processing software that searches documents for key words, a technology pioneered by the company Resumix but now offered by a number of vendors, just encourages job applicants to write their resumes to help them get selected by the software—sort of the way search engine technology has encouraged a movement to figure out how to stand out in searches. This software, then, is just one more reason why people are tempted to produce resumes that don't necessarily reflect the whole truth.

But for the moment, let's hold aside the fact that resumes are not particularly reliable as sources of background information. Even if they were completely true, it simply doesn't make sense to hire based on a piece of paper. Resumes merely list an individual's past positions, degrees attained, and affiliations. They say almost nothing about the traits that matter most when it comes to predicting people's workplace effectiveness—how they behave, their values, and what it is like to actually work with them, side by side, over long periods of time.

That kind of information is really hard to come by in our litigious society, where labor lawyers invariably counsel past employers to confirm only job title and dates of employment and maybe— just maybe—salary, for former employees. As one attorney told me, there is almost nothing to be gained by disclosing past issues or problems; and if the company is sued for libel, the costs, even if it prevails, are substantial. Why risk it? Ironically, resumes compound the problems by causing many job interviews to miss the mark. Much of an interview is often spent going over the applicant's background and asking questions about what is on the resume because that piece of paper is such a focus of attention.

A few years ago, I served on the board of a small software company that needed to hire a new CEO. We did what most companies do. We scrutinized resumes to see which of our applicants had the most impressive and relevant background. We were particularly taken with the credentials of one candidate—an MBA from a top business school who had held a senior position at a company that sold to the same target market—so, of course, our interviews focused mostly on "selling" the opportunity. The trouble is that showing up well in an interview is mostly based on looking good, sounding smart, and being verbally agile. Although nice skills to have, they are far from the most critical for managing people and building technology. Ultimately, we got precisely what we had interviewed for—experience on paper, smart talk, and great presentations—but sales stagnated and employee morale and product development were poor.

Focusing just on credentials and experience can be misleading because it can cause people to overestimate the ability of applicants. Remember the Peter Principle, the idea that people get promoted to their level of incompetence?[6] It may be that the person's last job is at the limit of his or her abilities, or maybe even one level beyond that, but you won't know that from just looking at what positions a job candidate has held.

And in other cases, credentials and the resume can cause companies to overlook valuable traits that transcend formal training and background. Neither Bill Gates nor Steve Jobs had stunning educational credentials—try no college degree—and neither had extensive, high-level work experience that might be required to preside as CEOs of two of the largest and most successful computer and software companies in the world. Steve Ballmer, CEO of Microsoft, dropped out of Stanford's MBA program. And one might assume that an entrepreneur from Stanford's computer science PhD program would concentrate on the technical dimensions of business. But when I had lunch with Google cofounder Larry Page a few years ago, he was mostly interested in talking about the company's organizational culture and how to maintain its vitality as it grew—"touchy-feely" concerns that he viewed as key to Google's continued success. Indeed, the company's fast-moving and wildly creative workplace remains an important source of its competitive advantage.

Resumes don't tell you about what drives people and what their essential nature is. Roger Martin, now the dean of the Rotman Business School at the University of Toronto, has an MBA from Harvard and had worked for years for Monitor, the strategy consulting firm. With no doctoral degree and no experience in academia, one might think that Martin would be a typical corporate-type dean who had little connection to or interest in the school's academic mission and research and would be mostly focused on public relations and fund-raising. But such an assumption would be completely wrong. Martin himself teaches—quite effectively—in Rotman's educational programs and since coming to Toronto has written numerous articles and a book.[7] He also leads a research project on the competitiveness of Ontario's economy. In fact, Martin, I dare say, has written more and been more engaged in research than many business school deans who *do* have PhDs and more academic backgrounds.

When Phil Satre, at the time the CEO of Harrah's Entertainment, hired Gary Loveman to become chief operating officer of the company in 1998, many people were surprised. Loveman was a 38-year-old untenured associate professor in the service management group at Harvard Business School, whose prior managerial experience had been supervising one-half of an administrative assistant (shared with another faculty member) and some research assistants. Loveman turned out to be incredibly successful in his new role, eventually becoming Harrah's CEO. As he told my class, he was always competitive and liked to win. It's just that he had chosen to compete in academia. But this drive, and his ability to communicate with others and teach them how to ask better and more thoughtful questions to analyze business problems, were precisely the attributes needed to help take Harrah's to the next level of performance. As his assistant told me, Loveman also has an amazing ability to relate to people at all levels, from Wall Street investment bankers to the dealers and cocktail servers in the casinos. This leadership skill has been instrumental in his success at Harrah's, but again, is not something that one can ascertain from examining a resume.

The U.S. Army has an interesting perspective on leaders and leadership, nicely captured in its slogan, "Be, Know, Do." Obviously, it is important to have the technical skills and experience to *do* the job—and these may be reflected on the resume. But basic values—the *being*—come first. The military recognizes that character is essential to a leader's nature, not something acquired by taking a class or holding a particular job title. In the post-Enron, post-Tyco, post-WorldCom era, that's an important lesson that corporations should have learned by now.

So how do you find out the truth beneath the resume? Many firms emphasize behavioral interviewing, asking people not to recount their accomplishments but to talk about how they might react to hypothetical situations, how they spend their free time, what they really enjoy and believe in, and how those values are reflected in their lives. Some companies assess their own values using a standardized instrument and then ask individuals to respond with their degree of agreement to the same list of values. Research has shown that individuals whose own values profile more closely matches that of their employing organization are likely to stay longer and be more successful.[8] Other organizations put people in simulated situations such as group decision-making exercises and see how they react, while others use work samples as an opportunity to gauge what people can and will do. And it is still possible to do due diligence on a hire, but probably not on the phone and certainly not without a lot of effort and digging.

Hiring people with real ability and leadership skills is actually a difficult but vital task for organizations of all sizes and types. It's not that difficult to find a smart-talking person with the perfect resume. But finding people who command respect and can successfully help others perform better are skills that are both rarer and more difficult to fake. Organizations would be well served to spend more time finding out who people really are and what they can do, and less time focusing on resumes. That's because in the end, resumes don't necessarily tell you a lot about the person.

Part III

Power Play

Rethinking Leadership and Influence

CHAPTER 14

The Courage to Rise Above
Don't Be Afraid to Stand Out

THERE'S AN INTERESTING THING about the leadership literature—for the most part, it tells you what to do once you have
already reached a high-level position, but for the most part it
doesn't say much about getting to that position in the first place.
And there is another issue also largely avoided by many discussions of leadership: the possibility that what is good in terms of
advancing an *individual's* career and interests may be inconsistent with what is good for the *organization's* long-term interests.
This point becomes clear when my MBA and executive students
comment that some of the material I teach on power and influence contradicts popular recommendations of people such as Jim
Collins in his discussion of "level 5 leadership"—that successful
leaders are not flashy or aggressive, but compassionate, consider-
ate, and modest.[1]

There is every reason to believe that just as leadership strategies and behavior may need to vary across different situations,
strategies and behavior may also need to differ over the course of
an individual's career and career stages. And we also need to keep
in mind that there are almost certainly trade-offs to be made, and

that there are not only trade-offs between individual and organizational interests but also choices to be made among various organizational objectives.

These issues come into sharp focus when we consider the question of how vigorously to pursue career ambitions and what strategies may be most effective for doing so. A lot of my Stanford MBA students, and for that matter, many faculty colleagues and even some business associates, believe that the road to success is paved by being nice (as well as smart, of course) and just doing good work. In class, students avoid arguing too vigorously with one another or criticizing each other's ideas. In a couple of self-diagnostic exercises in my Paths to Power course, students typically acknowledge not being particularly good or comfortable with tense or conflict-filled situations, and many don't even use bargaining as an influence strategy very often. They seem to believe that they'll have great careers if only they can develop reputations for getting along and not making too many waves. My job in this class is to convince them that life is a little more complex—that, in fact, if you don't do *anything* to stand out, it is unclear how you are going to differentiate yourself from your myriad competitors for promotions. And I also try to convince them that sometimes taking risks is important, even the risk of offending others.

One way I do this is by introducing them to the case of Keith Ferrazzi.[2] Currently running Ferrazzi Greenlight, his own marketing consulting and training firm, Ferrazzi, a kid from a working-class family in Pittsburgh, got his college degree at Yale and then earned his MBA at Harvard in 1992. He took his first job after business school at Deloitte Consulting and was in line to become partner when Starwood Hotels hired him as its chief marketing officer at the age of 32, making him the youngest CMO in a *Fortune* 500 company. In 2000, Ferrazzi became CEO of YaYa Media, a marketing and entertainment company that was using online gaming as a promotional strategy for various brands.

At YaYa, he doubled revenue each year—even during the dot-com implosion—and sold the company to American Vantage in 2003, at which point he founded Ferrazzi Greenlight.

Ferrazzi makes no attempt to mask his ambition and drive, and advises others to do the same. When he visited my class, he described his prodigious Rolodex—he is someone who has written a book on how to network, after all[3]—and recommended that students sort their contacts into A, B, and C lists based on their relevance to their own career goals. He noted that one could choose to associate—have dinner—with whomever one wanted, but that he preferred to spend a disproportionate amount of time associating with powerful and well-connected people who were both more interesting and could advance his career goals more effectively. He also advised the students to focus in their jobs on those activities they do well and stop worrying about trying to do every aspect of their assigned tasks effectively. Ferrazzi noted, relevant to this point, that he was neither particularly interested nor strong in the detailed analytics of consulting, so he managed, even as a young associate, to get others, including colleagues from Harvard Business School, to do that aspect of the work. Meanwhile, he never acted like a junior consultant. Instead, he focused on building external relationships and doing marketing and business development for Deloitte, activities that were much more important for the success of the firm than the consulting grunt work that others could and would do. For instance, he founded the Lincoln Award for Business Excellence (modeled on the Malcolm Baldrige Quality Award) in Illinois, making himself president and persuading top Chicago CEOs to serve as judges and board members.

Although the students are sometimes surprised by Ferrazzi's directness and honesty, and some are put off by his ambition and focus, they soon come to see how an overwhelming desire to not offend anyone, and to not stand out and possibly generate envy, can hamper career progress. For example, consider what Ferrazzi did when he graduated from Harvard Business School. With offers from both Deloitte and McKinsey, he told Deloitte he would accept their job on one condition: that he could dine with the CEO, Pat Loconto, at least three times a year. Deloitte agreed, and Loconto became both a friend and a valuable mentor. By the time he left Deloitte for Starwood, Ferrazzi sat on Deloitte's executive committee and had created a marketing and business development position for himself.

This story provides two important lessons. First, as Ferrazzi reminds people, contrary to much conventional wisdom, you are not solely responsible for your career. It is your bosses—those higher up in the corporate hierarchy—who have the power to promote you or not, and it is your job to ensure that they know you and have some reason to want to advance you over your competitors. Second, when asked how he had the nerve to make a request that might threaten peers and shock his future employer, Ferrazzi commented that it was a risk worth taking because the worst that could happen is that he would be turned down—nothing ventured, nothing gained. But if Deloitte accepted his request, he knew that both the acquiescence and the additional contact with senior leadership would provide him a visibility advantage over many of his peers. With all the talk about teamwork that is so in vogue today, it is nice to remember that colleagues aren't always on your side and are, in fact, competing for promotions and raises.

People are often reluctant to follow Ferrazzi's advice or example because they believe that upsetting others, taking too many chances, and standing out can come back to bite you. But although it is always possible that people may hold a grudge or try to bring down a high flyer, the downsides to following Ferrazzi's path are actually not that big if your goal is advancing your career and getting into a position of power. That's because Ferrazzi's strategy of standing out and being willing to ask for things and to take risks is well rooted in and supported by much social psychological research.

The first principle that his approach relies on is the idea of psychological commitment—the notion that once you do something for someone, particularly under little or no external pressure or inducement, the best way to make sense of that choice is to positively revalue that individual and to be psychologically invested in his or her success.[4] This tactic was used by Jimmy Carter, among many others. When Carter sought nomination for president as an outsider. he approached every Democrat who had lost a primary election in 1974 with a personal letter asking for their help. Carter realized that these people had time, and he offered them an opportunity to get involved, thereby binding them, through their efforts, to be interested in his success. When others do favors for you, when they comply with your requests for help, they will be more psychologically bound to you and your success and be even more willing to provide help in the future. Another example of this principle in action is asking others for career advice. Once others have provided you that advice and assistance, they are more committed to you and to your career success.

The second principle that helps make Ferrazzi's approach effective is that success causes others to want to join and associate with the successful person. This desire to be aligned with successful individuals and organizations helps people "forget" slights they may have suffered and their feelings of resentment. People do like to bask in reflected glory—for instance, one study found that students at a university were more likely to wear clothing with the school name or insignia on it on a Monday following a football victory on Saturday than they were if the team had lost that weekend.[5] Some people come to see even harsh and arbitrary treatment at the hands of bosses—vivid examples are described in *The Mailroom*, which chronicles early job experiences in Hollywood studios and talent agencies[6]—as a price to be paid for training, sponsorship, and getting a foot on the ladder of success—almost as some necessary rite of passage.

Moreover, prestige and status are contagious, in that the status of any given individual or company depends in part on the status of others in their social network—you are known by the company you keep.[7] Consequently, as long as Ferrazzi keeps doing well, the idea of people being harshly judgmental seems unlikely.

The third principle that makes Ferrazzi's strategy successful is that the passage of time causes us to selectively remember events and people. To avoid being perpetually unhappy, we tend to remember positive things more than negative ones and to put a more positive gloss on events from the past. And, in addition, our memory is to a considerable extent under the influence of our motives. If we have a reason to want to like someone—that person is now successful and in a position to provide help—our memory will help our liking by selectively recalling more positive rather than negative aspects of past interactions.

And the fourth principle reprises Ferrazzi's perceptive comment that those who matter most to your career success are those higher up in organizations. When Henry Kissinger was a student in the government department at Harvard, his arrogance alienated many of his peers. But his ability to develop close mentorship relations with two powerful senior faculty in the department, who themselves were feuding with each other, provided the sponsorship to get a position in the department on his graduation.[8] Similarly, biographies of President Lyndon Johnson describe him in his early years on Capitol Hill—first as a congressional secretary and subsequently as a representative and then a junior senator—as a "professional son," skilled at building relationships with senior, powerful people such as Senator Richard Russell and House Speaker Sam Rayburn, even as his behavior often distanced him from his contemporaries.[9]

Many people achieve some degree of success by being a standout in, but remaining one of, the crowd. Doing things to *really*

stand out—to push your own career and success, to build relationships with people in power—almost inevitably means that
some people will envy or even dislike you. But that may be a price
that at least some are willing to pay for success. After all, as Steve
Spurrier, the very successful University of Florida football coach,
remarked in an interview around the time he was preparing to
announce his move to coach in the National Football League,
"Call me arrogant, cocky, crybaby, whiner, or whatever names you
like . . . At least they're not calling us losers anymore. If people
like you too much, it's probably because they're beating you."[10]

CHAPTER 15

Executive-in-Chief

The Importance of Framing and Repetition

REGARDLESS OF YOUR political persuasion or what you think of the job George W. Bush has done as president, there are important lessons on leadership to be gleaned by considering how he has communicated his message to the American people. These lessons, applicable to any organization, public or private, helped Bush win reelection in 2004 with the largest popular vote in history, and helped him and his colleagues put his opponents on the defensive on issues ranging from the Iraq war to tax cuts. Yes, the Republicans suffered serious setbacks in the 2006 Congressional elections and Bush's job approval ratings have fallen throughout his second term, but I would argue that you have to put his relative "success" in context. In the face of the Iraq debacle, rampant economic insecurity among the middle class, and Bush's confrontational style—not to mention that of his vice president and secretary of defense—the level of support he has achieved and maintained is really stunning.

But in any event, as our first president with an MBA degree (from Harvard Business School), his management approach has elements that a number of senior executives employ and things that are generally considered to be sound ideas for developing and exercising power and influence in settings where there is interpersonal competition and the need to get things done. Here are four of the most general and most important lessons, and their implications for managers everywhere.

DEFINING THE CRITERIA FOR SUCCESS

You can—and should—actively define and determine the dimensions of job performance that you believe matter most, and on which you score the highest. Do not presume there is some "objective reality" on which everyone agrees and a set of measures that everyone naturally uses. John Kotter, in his course on power and influence at the Harvard Business School, would tell the students that their boss would not necessarily know what they had accomplished, so it was their responsibility to bring their performance to the boss's attention. And because it was likely that the boss and employee would not necessarily have identical views of the employee's role, it was also the employee's responsibility to proactively (1) ensure that he or she understood how the boss defined success and (2) ensure that the boss saw the contributions the employee was making along those dimensions.

In the case of the Bush presidency, there is virtually no dispute that neither the war in Iraq nor the economy went as well as the president and his advisers would have liked. But in the end, those setbacks, and even the soaring budget and trade deficits, did not matter as much as they might have. Bush defined the performance criteria differently—contrasting what did occur with what might have happened had he not acted by invading Iraq and by passing large tax cuts (including a cut in the estate tax that received very high support in public opinion polls even though it affects very few people). And he focused the discussion of his job, and therefore its evaluation, almost strictly on the "war on terror," an interesting metaphor that itself has implications for the dimensions used to evaluate his performance.

Corporate examples of defining and redefining criteria for success abound. Consider General Motors' CEO, Rick Wagoner. Although GM has lost market share for years in the crucial U.S. market and has rung up enormous financial losses, in a speech to 250 journalists before the North American International Auto Show, Wagoner touted GM's growth in the Asia-Pacific region. And even though GM was losing money in Europe, Wagoner reminded the audience that GM's performance there "was the best in five years."[1]

Or consider media figure Tina Brown, the British-born editor first of *Vanity Fair*, then the *New Yorker*, and finally the now-defunct *Talk* magazine. Although Brown's magazines apparently never were profitable, she increased circulation dramatically at both *Vanity Fair* and the *New Yorker* and made both publications topics of conversation in the highest circles of government and industry. Brown defined performance by the quality of the magazine product and by the circulation and buzz produced, not necessarily by profits.[2] After *Talk* folded, Brown appeared on NBC's *Today Show* to be interviewed by Matt Lauer. In spite of Lauer's persistent attempts to get her to admit to a failed business model or other mistakes, she reaffirmed her pride in the quality of what the team had accomplished, attributed the problems that caused the magazine to close to the economy and insufficient financial backing, and noted that even in the difficult environment of the early 2000s, advertising revenues were up. Brown also noted that every career has setbacks. She was able to define success on her terms, and more importantly, define the criteria for success in a way that left those who worked with her on the magazines feeling proud of what they had accomplished.

PROJECTING CLARITY AND CONFIDENCE

A leader's job is to reduce uncertainty, not create it, for those around him or her, and to project confidence that the task ahead is, in fact, doable. I frankly don't like the way that many politicians, and for that matter corporate executives, tend to oversimplify complex problems and persist in the pursuit of failing strategies that have little hope of eventual success. But doubts and complexities are often best left to private deliberations. People need to be told the truth about the situation, because otherwise leaders lose credibility and also show disrespect for the intelligence of their audience. But people also need and want to be told that truth with the assurance that the person doing the telling has the individuals' interests at heart and knows what to do to further those interests and create success. If people believe that success is possible, they will commit their efforts and therefore increase the odds of being successful. If they think failure is on the horizon, they will engage in preemptory surrender, thereby making failure a more likely outcome. This is yet another example of the self-fulfilling prophecy in action.

Steve Jobs, the founder of animation studio Pixar and co-founder of Apple Computer, is famous for his ability to create a so-called "reality distortion field" in which people believe in the reality he articulates. This ability to inspire confidence through effective communication is a skill that literally kept Apple alive in the early 1980s. With IBM having entered the personal computer market and with the market failure of the Lisa computer, Jobs faced a tough task in introducing the new Macintosh in 1984. If people believed the computer—and the company—would fail, no one write software for it and no one would buy it. Jobs's ability to project the Macintosh as a revolutionary new computer that would change the world of personal computing made that reality come true.[3]

I saw this lesson of instilling confidence while being truthful in an effort to produce better results put into practice firsthand in the mid-1980s. I watched Dr. Frances K. Conley, the first female neurosurgeon and a full professor at Stanford Medical School, talk to a patient with a malignant brain tumor. When talking with her surgical fellows, Conley was justifiably uncertain about the best course of treatment, but when she walked into the patient's room, although she did not downplay the seriousness of the situation, she also laid out the course of action she recommended. When I subsequently asked her about the difference in her demeanor in the two settings, she replied that with the people she was training, it was important to discuss the many uncertainties and contingencies of treatment. But in dealing with patients, it was important to provide some sense of reassurance even while being honest about the difficulty of the situation. If patients felt more positive about their prospects, the placebo effect might increase their chance of recovery, their outlook would improve because of the connection between the mind and body, and they were more likely to carry through with the recommended treatment.

In an interview with Clayton Christensen, Andy Grove, co-founder and former CEO and chairman of the board of Intel, spoke of the importance of projecting confidence even in uncertain situations:

> None of us have a real understanding of where we're heading. I don't . . . Part of it is self-discipline and part of it is deception. And the deception becomes reality. Deception in the sense that you pump yourself up and put a better face on things than you start off feeling. But after a while, if you act confident, you become more confident. So the deception becomes less of a deception.[4]

Grove recognized that even under conditions of uncertainty, decisions needed to get made. What you do as a leader is make the best decisions you can at the time and clean up the bad decisions later.

Moving First to Establish the Terms of the Discussion

If you are able to determine the language that will be used to frame an issue and the criteria that are going to be used to decide it, you will have largely succeeded in exercising a tremendous amount of influence. Consider, for example, the question of changing strategy in the Iraq war. When Bush ran against John Kerry in 2004, the debate over the war became defined in terms of "staying the course" versus "flip-flopping," and later as one of "achieving success" versus "cut and run." No one wants to be considered a flip-flopper or someone uninterested in being successful, and staying the course sounds like sensible patience in the face of inevitable setbacks. And, the Bush campaign asked questions about whether Kerry was as much a war hero as he claimed he was, thereby diverting attention from the fact that Bush had served in the National Guard—apparently with an undistinguished record—and had no firsthand battle experience at all.

I served on the board of a human resources software company that was cutting its prices because of competitive pressure as licensing contracts got renewed. One could plausibly argue that the price cutting was caused by the company's inability to get new product features completed in a timely fashion, its ineffective marketing and sales efforts, and its failure to sufficiently differentiate its offerings—all of which had let the competitors in the marketplace get a strong foothold. But this was not the language used by our incredibly skillful CEO to describe our contract renewals. He argued that although we were giving substantial price concessions before contracts were up for renewal at some of our larger clients—a move that cut revenues and adversely affected profits—this was a prudent move to "lock up our long-term clients" and ensure a solid future with a secure contract backlog. The discussion of why we needed to actually reduce our price to lock up the deals got lost in the "triumph" of securing a big, albeit lower margin, backlog.

ENDLESSLY REPEATING SIMPLE MESSAGES

As Jack Welch has reportedly said, building or changing an organizational culture requires being "relentless and boring." If you think you have told people something enough, you probably haven't. That's because people forget what to do and forget why they're doing it. After a while, something repeated frequently enough becomes accepted as true, even if it isn't. President Bush tied the war in Iraq to the September 11 attack on the World Trade Center. Even though no weapons of mass destruction were ever found in Iraq, and even though there is no evidence of a connection between Iraq and the attacks on the Twin Towers, the repetition of this message caused about 50 percent of the people responding to public opinion polls to see Iraq and 9/11 as connected, even five years later. The point: people will come to believe things if they are repeated. And simple messages are easier to remember.

At Wells Fargo Bank, CEO Richard Kovacevich has been repeating the same strategy and theme he articulated years ago when he was CEO at Norwest until, as he puts it, people can repeat it in their sleep: to "outnational" local banks by offering a broader range of products and services, and to "outlocal" national banks by offering better and more personalized customer service.

The overarching lesson is a simple one. Leadership is, in part, about effective communication. Employees, just like voters, spend their days bombarded by cell-phone calls, e-mail messages, and video programming, so getting their attention focused on what is important and what they should do can be difficult. Time and again, Bush's easy-to-understand, repetitious messages have proven to be effective weapons in the battle for public opinion, as has his ability to define the terms and issues of the debate and to project assurance and confidence even when things aren't going well. No matter what you think about these political strategies, leaders would be well-served to learn the lessons of how well and why they work.

CHAPTER 16

How to Turn On the Charm

Building Influence Through Real
Human Interaction for a Change

WHAT EVER HAPPENED to manners? Every week a handful of my students arrive to class late and disrupt the discussion as they make their way to their seats. Or they come and go during the session to get coffee or food or to use their cell phones. And some come to class unprepared. But MBA candidates behave no more rudely than many executives I encounter in the corporate world. Executives also arrive at meetings late, even when this late arrival could have been avoided. At some board meetings I attend, a few directors invariably haul out their BlackBerries to answer messages and thumb out e-mails. I've seen executives and directors take cell-phone calls during meetings and actually leave the meeting to attend to the call. At dozens of companies, I've seen bosses looking through papers or at their personal digital assistants while talking to employees, and I've heard about workers reading their e-mails or surfing the Internet during phone conversations. On company conference calls, I've listened as investment analysts join the call 30 minutes late and then ask questions that have already been discussed, with not a word of apology for wasting everyone's time.

Manners seem to be in short supply in today's busy world. It's as if some new form of attention deficit disorder has overtaken the workplace, and the idea of focusing on one thing or one person at a time seems somehow quaint and outdated, while showing up on time is strictly optional. Meanwhile, I get all kinds of e-mailed requests, including requests for meetings and assistance, from people I don't know—apparently personal, face-to-face communication also seems to be something that is seriously out of fashion.

But all this behavior is completely counterproductive to getting things done—which invariably requires building and exercising influence—in a world filled with interdependence with other people. That's because if your bosses or colleagues are "multitasking" while you are speaking with them, they have sent a powerful and direct message: you're just not as important as the next e-mail or phone call. If people can't spend the time to meet with you personally, the message is that other activities have higher priority. And that's a bad signal to send. If there is one thing people care about, it is being taken seriously and treated as if they are important. So, behavior that treats others with discourtesy and disrespect is certainly no way to win friends.

As Robert Cialdini pointed out in his best-selling book, *Influence: The Psychology of Persuasion*, courtesy is important as an influence technique because people are much more likely to do things for—and accede to requests from—people they like.[1] We are more likely to feel warmly toward people who flatter us and make us feel good about ourselves, and one of the best ways of flattering someone is paying attention to that individual. So, mastering the art of being likeable is a crucial skill for leaders or for those who aspire to leadership positions.

My friends in high technology, addicted to their electronic gadgets and multitasking, could learn a lot by watching Jack Valenti in action. Valenti, for those who don't know, was an advertising executive running his own agency in Texas who became an aide to President Lyndon Johnson in late 1963. In 1966, Valenti left this job to become head of the Motion Picture Association of America, the organization that represents the economic and political interests of the major motion picture studios. That job is both tough and political. As head of the MPAA, Valenti had to keep the studio heads, people with colossal egos and often conflicting economic interests, happy. Nonetheless, Valenti held the job for more than 38 years—until he was in his 80s.

While Valenti ran the organization, the MPAA was typically rated as the best or second-best lobbying organization in Washington. Valenti handled relations with Congress concerning such touchy issues as sex and violence in the movies—he came up with the industry-administered parental rating system—censorship, and most recently, protecting digital content such as movies from electronic piracy. In the conflict during the 1990s between the MPAA and the technology industry over copyright protection and the electronic distribution of content, the general assessment is that the MPAA emerged victorious. When Valenti announced he was stepping down, technology columnist John Heilemann wrote that Valenti was formidable and had become the Silicon Valley's "public-policy bête noire."[2] Success in lobbying for the movie industry, as would be the case for any lobbying effort, came in no small measure because of Valenti's skill in building and maintaining relationships with powerful people in Congress and the media.[3]

The keys to his power and relationship-building skills are easily observed. Jack has been kind enough to occasionally visit my MBA elective on power in organizations, and I have had the opportunity to see him work his magic firsthand as well as hear him describe his modus operandi to the class. The lessons are at once simple but also frequently ignored in a world in which everyone seems to be too busy to engage in direct, personal contact characterized by charm and manners.

The first and possibly most important principle is to be consistently polite and to put yourself in the other person's place. That entails returning phone calls, from senators and representatives of course, but even from congressional staffers, personally—not by an assistant—and typically within 24 hours. Valenti recalls his early days, going to college while he also worked to support himself, and says he has never forgotten the help and encouragement he received. He believes, and more importantly, acts, as if everyone he comes in contact with is someone worthy of dignity and respect. Many of the people with real power, such as the control over calendars and access, don't necessarily have prominent job titles. But Valenti's consistent courtesy and charming demeanor have built relationships up and down the corridors of power, serving him in very good stead.

Many other highly successful executives—Warren Buffett, Colgate's Reuben Mark, DaVita's Kent Thiry—likewise use personal courtesy and virtuoso listening skills as strategic weapons. All of them make whomever they're listening to feel like the center of the universe at that moment, and the payoff is fierce loyalty. As UBS stock analyst Andrew McQuilling, who has followed Colgate for several years, has said of CEO Mark, "His employees would take a bullet for him."[4]

The second principle is, to the extent possible, do business in person, possibly over the phone—but certainly never try to conduct serious discussions using e-mail. Valenti's wife never wanted to move to California, so he has maintained a home in Washington as well as one in Los Angeles. He travels frequently between the two, because whether he is meeting with studio executives and other people from the entertainment industry in Hollywood, or legislators in Washington, Valenti believes that personal contact—being physically present—is essential in forging the sort of ties that one can count on in a pinch. The movie industry sells its entertainment products all over the world, and there are many cultural sensitivities and concerns about the dominance of U.S.-created entertainment in countries such as France. Valenti has traveled tirelessly to countries ranging from France to China to

India, in the process building personal ties with important political and corporate figures—ties founded on a personal connection born of face-to-face contact—that have helped protect the film industry from excessive tariffs or exclusionary policies.

The importance of personal contact is a lesson not lost on Larry Culp, the CEO of Danaher, an industrial company that has made more than 50 acquisitions since early 2000.[5] Culp meets personally with the leaders of companies he might be interested in acquiring, traveling all over the country to do so. In building that personal rapport, he helps build trust and avoid bidding wars that might drive the price up to an unacceptable level. Many sellers of companies are interested in more than just getting the highest price; they also want to be sure that their business is going to be in the hands of people who will take care of it and their employees. That sort of reassurance is much easier to convey in person.

Third, Valenti instinctively knows that one of the best ways to build a relationship is to find some way in which you share something in common with the person you are talking to. Research has shown that people are more willing to do favors and extend themselves for people with whom they share a social identity, even if what they have in common is not something as consequential as where they went to school but as casual and random as having the same birthday.[6] So when MBA students from my course would come up to meet him, Valenti would ask about where they were from or where they had worked, or what their career aspirations were. In each instance, he would talk about knowing someone from their hometown, or having some connection to the company or industry that they had once been employed in, or how his own career had something in common with what they were seeking to do. This effort permitted him, extremely quickly, to make a personal connection with each student.

Fourth, Valenti understands, and uses, the power of flattery. Complimenting people works quite well to increase likeability.

That's because of the self-enhancement motive—our desire to feel good about ourselves and our accomplishments. We like people who help us do that. People often underestimate the power of flattery, because we think we won't be taken in. But we are motivated to believe the compliments are sincere. If someone compliments you on your ability or job performance, you can have two reactions. On the one hand, you can presume the comment is meant only to be ingratiating and discount it. That, however, leaves you feeling bad about yourself—the other person must believe you are quite gullible—and also feeling bad about that other person's devious behavior. Or on the other hand, you can believe that the compliment was sincerely offered, and that the individual making the flattering statement is just an unusually astute observer of human character and behavior. This alternative will leave you feeling better about yourself, for having been complimented, and about the person making the nice statement. Given the motivational desire to feel better rather than worse, the odds are you are going to not look a "gift compliment" in the mouth or subject it to too much scrutiny.

Jack Valenti flattered Lyndon Johnson, complimenting him on his political skills and also on his accomplishments, energy, and judgments.[7] As part and parcel of his gracious persona, he has complimented my students on their accomplishments and attainments—for instance by noting that he is flattered that people of their intelligence and professional stature would deign to come to the auditorium where he was talking rather than be somewhere else. And, in a wonderful turn of phrase, when I wrote him a letter thanking him for his appearance and for the wonderful lessons he imparted, he complimented me for my skills in offering thanks, writing "what a gracious, graceful letter."[8]

The incorrigible multitasker will argue that there isn't enough time to personally answer so many phone calls and take so many meetings in person, that e-mail is much more efficient, and there are so many things that need to be done that doing a bunch of them simultaneously saves time. I don't buy it for a minute. If you are constantly giving people the message that they aren't important enough to get your full attention, it will take you longer to get things done with and through them when you find yourself dependent on them. And you might consider how much time you spend *avoiding* people, compared with the brief moment it would take to pay attention to someone, one time. And that one brief interaction, effectively handled, can make a colleague or acquaintance a lifetime ally.

CHAPTER 17

A Field Day for Executives

*The Benefits of Knowing What
Your Organization Actually Does*

IN THE SPRING OF 2004 my wife and I flew into Newark airport on a Continental Airlines flight from Madrid. We had an airline-scheduled window of a little less than two hours to make a connecting flight to San Francisco, but 70 minutes later, in the crowded international baggage arrivals hall, our suitcases had yet to appear. During our wait, we observed a phenomenon all too common in many corporations: customer-facing employees scrambling to make up for management misjudgments. Continental ground personnel were doing their best to calm irate passengers waiting interminably for their luggage and book new connecting flights for those who were missing their scheduled connections, all the while providing cheerful, professional service. This customer service heroism, displayed on an almost daily basis according to a few of the employees we talked to, was made necessary by some genius at corporate headquarters who had decided that more than half of Continental's flights from Europe—at that time 13 wide-body aircraft, most of them full—should arrive between 12:30 and 2:30 p.m, creating a peak load spike in work that the ground personnel simply couldn't handle, regardless of their efforts.

In case you haven't noticed, airline employees seem to be continually apologizing for decisions made by higher-ups—awful food or no food at all, little legroom, no pillows and blankets, no magazines, poor scheduling—but they're hardly the only people who find themselves in this position. Help desk personnel at software companies make excuses for buggy software. Call center staff at mail-order companies have to explain order fulfillment gaffes and product quality problems. Nurses and physicians find themselves answering for the difficulties created by health-insurance policies drafted by people who never see patients.

At the turn of the twentieth century, Frederick Taylor and the scientific management movement began what has become an inexorable march toward separating the planning of work from its doing. It has become almost axiomatic in today's corporations that status is measured by how far you are from the actual work of the organization—like the vice president of Macy's West. A Macy's employee told me how, when this august personage visited the store, he did not deign to greet customers or employees but went straight to the private meeting room to be briefed on the store's merchandising strategies. In the typical company, it is amazing how little contact senior management typically has with daily operations.

This sorry state of affairs leaves executives hopelessly out of touch and unable to empathize with or even understand the situation faced by front-line staff. Being removed from the front lines also flies in the face of the wisdom of Honda, which years ago, as it taught its U.S. suppliers how to improve quality, revealed one of its keys to success: its problem-solving motto "actual part, actual place, actual situation." Honda understood that when you sat in a meeting room discussing some problem—for instance, with the paint finish—you necessarily dealt with an abstraction of the real situation on the shop floor. No matter how well-intentioned and well-motivated people are, it's inevitable that if they're not where problems occur they will forget or overlook seemingly small details that could prove crucial to actually fixing the trouble. That's why Honda recommended that people go to site of the problem—to the place on the factory floor where the paint was applied, in our example—to experience and see the problem firsthand.[1]

It is imperative that executives who are going to make decisions about situations and lead people who work in their companies have firsthand experience with what the company does. Promotion from within is useful in this regard—it is beneficial for those at the top to actually know something about the business they are leading. But outside hiring of senior executive talent is increasing, and fewer and fewer people actually start in front-line positions before acceding to the senior executive ranks. And even in case of promotion from within, memories can be short, particularly when the new executives are surrounded by the perquisites of high corporate status.

That's why some companies—albeit not enough of them—do something quite simple to provide executives with a sense of what it is like to do the organization's work: they have those executives actually *do* that work—not just visit and chat with employees, but actually do the job—for some period of time. At Southwest Airlines, this program is called a "day in the field"; and once a quarter, senior leaders are expected to do a front-line job such as answering calls, handling baggage, checking passengers in, or serving as flight attendants. At Men's Wearhouse, the off-price retailer of tailored men's clothing, regional managers and senior executives are encouraged to visit stores regularly and, if they are in the store and a customer needs attention, to wait on that customer. AES, the independent power producer, used to have a program in which senior leaders, including the CEO, would spend a week working at a power plant. Once, when we checked in at the Regent Hotel in Sydney, Australia, the person at the front desk apologized for being less-than-proficient at her task. As she explained, she was normally in accounting but the Regent had a program to make sure that all people, including those in support or back-office roles, had occasional experience with the guests who were the hotel's bread and butter.

DaVita, the second-largest provider of kidney dialysis services in the United States, has a program called "Reality 101." Anyone being hired in from the outside or promoted to a position of vice president or above must spend a week working in a dialysis center, interacting with patients and staff and seeing what it is like to get up at 4 a.m. and be at the center by 5 so that it can be set up and open for its first patients at 6. Their chief of information technology showed me, some years later, copies of patient treatment records he had filled out during that week and proudly told me about actually inserting needles into patients. These front-line experiences provide an appreciation for the work and its many subtle complexities that would be otherwise missed.

And working on the front lines can even help provide information that is useful for improving procedures. Take Kathryn Clubb, formerly a senior partner at Accenture, who early in her career worked as a financial analyst at Northwest Airlines. As the airline sought to keep operating during a strike by ground personnel, managers and analysts were thrown into the breach and expected to do jobs temporarily vacated by striking employees. Clubb spent time loading and unloading baggage, which, she says, helped her design more efficient baggage-handling procedures.

Companies benefit in another way from having their executives occasionally do front-line work. Word of such behavior gets around and builds enormous credibility with the workforce. Similarity, an important basis of interpersonal attraction, is created in part through shared experiences. Employees will believe that a senior executive who has actually done their job will understand what they face and empathize with them more, so they will trust executive decisions to a greater degree. And executives, knowing more about the actual operations of the organization, will be able to answer more questions and speak more knowledgeably about organizational issues.

Critics occasionally point out a couple of downsides to days in the field for senior executives—or for that matter, boards of directors—but I don't find either argument compelling. The first is that having senior executives, who probably aren't as proficient with the front-line tasks, do that work instills some inefficiency into work processes. Although this is invariably true—I am sure DaVita senior leaders are less proficient in the tasks in the dialysis centers than the people who do them every day—learning anything always requires the expenditure of resources. Learning isn't free. If you want yourself and your colleagues to know what the front-line work is like, doing it for a while seems like a small price to pay.

The other criticism concerns the potential of this practice to disrupt the lines of authority. After all, while senior Men's Wearhouse executives are in-store, wardrobe consultants or tailors may confide things about their district-level or regional managers that those folks would prefer to have not disclosed. But I actually think this is an upside. The big problem that senior leaders face is not knowing what is actually going on, and many things conspire to ensure that they hear only good news, carefully scripted. If you believe, as I do, that fixing problems and making things better requires more accurate information, cultivating input from multiple sources, including front-line employees, would seem to be a useful first step. If people fear communication between front-line staff and senior leadership, that fear probably reflects some deficiencies in leadership that need to be fixed.

Of course, one of the privileges of rising in an organization is graduating from the demands of grunt work. And it would be impossible for leaders to spend all their time serving customers or producing or designing the company's products. But more organizations should follow the lead of Men's Wearhouse, DaVita, Southwest Airlines, and Honda. By doing the work, leaders build more credibility with those they lead through the experiences they share. And managers develop insight and understanding that can only come through direct experience.

Direct experience might have changed Continental Airlines' behavior. I'll bet that after spending one week in baggage claim at Newark's Continental international arrivals terminal, the airline's scheduling gurus—or even its directors—exhausted and fed up with angry and frustrated travelers and exposed firsthand to the stress the company's employees experience daily—might find a way to expand the flight arrival window beyond 120 minutes.

CHAPTER 18

The Whole Truth, and Nothing But

TRUTH IS AN ENDANGERED SPECIES inside many contemporary organizations. People who surface problems or issues are often told that they aren't "team players" or are being "too negative." And the old adage about killing the messenger, or at least resenting the messenger, still holds. Ken Lay and Jeff Skilling clearly did not want to hear about the problems that might cause Enron to miss its financial projections. So Sherron Watkins was basically told to leave the company after she brought the unwelcome information to Lay's attention, while Andrew Fastow was rewarded handsomely for massaging the numbers. But it's not just in places like Enron. This tendency to want to hear good news is extremely widespread, and organizational leaders signal in a variety of subtle and less subtle ways that they want to be told what they want to hear. Or as the line from the Fleetwood Mac song goes, "tell me lies, tell me sweet little lies."

Between the layers of hierarchy that filter information in large organizations, and the tendency to pass only good information upwards, or at least to put a more positive gloss on what does get passed up the line, most CEOs don't know what is actually going on inside their organizations. Ignorance of the facts makes managing effectively essentially impossible and can even cost lives. Following the explosion of the *Challenger* space shuttle, the Rogers Commission investigated how the shuttle could have been launched when there were long-standing and widely shared concerns on the part of many engineers about the effects of the cold temperatures on the safety of the engine. Physicist Richard Feynman, who served on that commission, provided one answer: when he asked a group of engineers to estimate the probability that the shuttle's main engine would fail, their estimates ranged between 1 in 200 and 1 in 300. The comparable estimate from higher-ups: 1 in 100,000.[1]

Of course, it doesn't have to be this way. Gary Loveman, CEO of Harrah's Entertainment, the world's largest casino gaming company, has built a culture where it is facts and evidence that drive decision making—and where telling the truth and admitting mistakes is the best road to success. When Loveman visited my class, he told about visiting a casino that was not performing well and being told that yes, performance wasn't good, but the casino leaders knew what to do. It's news the boss wants to hear—he can get back on the corporate jet and doesn't have to deliver bad news to his bosses, the board of directors. Months later, nothing had changed. Loveman came down hard on those folks, hoping to send a message throughout the company that covering up problems was not a good idea. It must have worked. When Loveman later visited another troubled casino, its leaders told him what they had tried to do and why they had done it, but admitted that nothing was working and that they were basically clueless about what to try next. Loveman praised them. As he noted, what's the point of having a corporate staff and some 30 separate operating sites if you aren't going to bring the resources, knowledge, and insight from the staff and other locations to help an underperforming asset? But in order to provide help, you first need to know there is a problem, and that requires having people in the company who are willing, and comfortable enough, to tell the truth.

The best way to inject an organization with truth serum is to start at the top. When leaders admit that they don't know everything, that they too make mistakes, and that they are completely comfortable with talking about those mistakes and telling the truth about what is going right and what is going wrong, they set an example that others are likely to follow. So, when Loveman made a decision about Harrah's health care plans that was both costly and inconvenient to the employees, he faced the facts. He went around the company getting in front of as many people as he could; apologized for the mistake; noted that he was trying to fix it; and also admitted that the mistake wasn't human resources' or the company's, it was his. As he noted, senior people and those in public relations get nervous about this behavior, but Loveman maintained that the only way to run a business is to know what is really going on and the only way to know what is going on is to build a culture of truth-telling—and this behavior has to start at the top.

Admitting mistakes is rare in corporations.[2] Studies that content-analyzed annual reports show that the aphorism, "success has many parents but failure is an orphan," is empirically true. In many instances, when the company did well, credit went to its strategy and its leadership. When things didn't go well, external factors, ranging from the general economy to commodity prices to fluctuations in foreign exchange rates, got the blame.[3] So, Air Canada's CEO Robert Milton, when the company filed for bankruptcy in April 2003, blamed everything from Canadian airports to the government of Dubai and the carrier's labor unions for the company's problems.

But that's not a very effective way to run an organization. It might make sense to admit mistakes just like Gary Loveman did. Fiona Lee and Larissa Tiedens found that companies' stock prices were higher one year later when they blamed poor performance on controllable internal factors rather than on external events that people could not do anything about.[4] Numerous studies have also shown that making excuses is an ineffective customer service strategy. Consumers value an admission of failure and an apology—in fact, it's the single most important thing in their assessment of service recovery efforts. Once a service failure has occurred, customers want to deal with people who are empowered to solve their problems, not hear that someone else—sometimes the customer!—is to blame.[5]

Admitting errors not only helps in building a culture of telling the truth, it also helps mobilize effort. Morale suffers when people don't believe that their own actions affect their organization's performance. Attributing problems to forces outside of anyone's control fuels a culture of helplessness. Admitting mistakes, on the other hand, is the first step toward recovery. No one in a company is going to fix a problem until executives name and describe it. No one will feel like taking responsibility for his or her own mistakes unless he sees the company's leaders doing the same thing.

Anne Mulcahy became CEO of Xerox in 2001. After just five months on the job she told Wall Street that the company's business model was flawed. Then she explained to employees, directly and honestly, the challenges they faced—the first step in creating a remarkable turnaround at Xerox. That unexpected honesty told employees that the person in charge actually knew and was willing to talk about the truth and had a plan for making things better. Hospitals in the United States are now forced by law to admit their errors. And research shows that doing so defuses anger and even results in fewer malpractice suits than attempts to deny problems or cover up mistakes.[6]

Creating a culture where people feel free to admit they need help, where they have an attitude of wisdom—knowing what they know and knowing what they don't know—also requires CEOs and other senior leaders to stop bluffing their way through situations. Instead of making stuff up, admit what you don't know when asked a question, and promise to find out. That's precisely the approach that Kent Thiry, CEO of kidney dialysis company DaVita does. At every employee gathering he or other leaders attend, it is a requirement that there be a "town meeting" where employees are free to ask any question they want. Now obviously some of those questions involve details that Thiry may not be familiar with. His response, even in front of 440 front-line employees, is "I don't know, I'll have to get back to you on that." And he makes it his business to find out the answer and respond. This behavior creates an environment in which people can admit their own uncertainties and what they don't know. And this is the first step toward learning. After all, you are only going to be committed to learning if you feel a need to learn—and that means understanding and admitting what you don't know.

Everyone makes mistakes. No one can know everything. And some bad news is inevitable—not everything goes perfectly all the time. As hindsight has shown, companies that consistently "made" their numbers for Wall Street frequently did so by literally making things up or taking various accounting liberties. Nothing in business is completely predictable or assured.

So the next time you're listening to a senior organizational leader, or for that matter, watching someone on the nightly news, watch that person's behavior. Does he or she admit to not knowing something, the first step toward learning? Admit mistakes? And tell the truth, to the best of his or her ability, or is it "all spin, all the time"? The research literature and logic is quite clear—good management requires telling the truth, asking for help, and learning. Building a culture where people are rewarded for identifying problems and telling the truth—and even better, for suggesting solutions—isn't easy, as it goes against the natural human tendencies to like those who agree with us and to prefer happy talk, even if it isn't true. But truth telling and admissions of ignorance are crucial requirements for long-term business success.

CHAPTER 19

Refuse to Lose

Persistence Pays

AT THE CLOSING DINNER for the sale of a company on whose board I sat, a venture capitalist friend commented to another VC that he had passed on an investment opportunity in a human capital software company, a decision that he now regretted. He noted that the company sold what appeared to be a poor product with a bad record of sales momentum into a very competitive and difficult market space, but the firm had succeeded in spite of all of that because of its management. Of course management matters. But the aphorism that you are better off betting on a good team in a poor market than an ineffective team in a great market, while valid, is too broad. Rather, the specific lesson is to be found in what made that particular company, Success Factors, a winner—nothing other than dogged persistence.

As leaders look to hire talent, a lot of emphasis is placed on finding people who are smart and well educated. And much of the literature supports this view.[1] Indeed, my students think that their high level of intellectual skill will be all they need to make them successful—that coupled with their connections and the Stanford brand. But both people doing hiring and those concerned with their own careers often overlook the importance of determination and resilience in creating successful business outcomes.

Determination or persistence, for either a company or an individual, does *not* mean simply continuing to do what has not worked in the past. Success requires learning and adaptation. What persistence entails is the quality of not giving up, of being able to make something out of nothing, of continually adjusting one's tactics and strategies but remaining on course, and in the process surmounting setbacks and obstacles.

Persistence and resilience are often hallmarks of successful careers, although we—and those successful individuals—often like to rewrite history and forget about the setbacks and disappointments that had to be surmounted for these people to attain their positions. Eliot Spitzer, New York State's attorney general, won the governor's race overwhelmingly in 2006 after making a name for himself suing mutual funds, insurance brokers, and investment firms for taking advantage of customers and investors. But the first time he ran in the Democratic primary for AG in 1994, he came in dead last.[2] Willie Brown, the two-term mayor of San Francisco, served for 16 years as speaker of the California Assembly before running up against term limits and is considered to be one of the most successful and powerful black—or for that matter, any—politicians in the history of the state. The first time he ran for election to the Assembly, he lost. And the first time he sought the post of speaker, he was soundly defeated.[3] Ronald Reagan, the iconic two-term president of the United States who won reelection by carrying every state but one, lost the first time he sought the presidential nomination. Jimmy Carter, defeated in his bid for a second term as president, went on to greatness as an ex-president, winning the Nobel Peace Prize for his work with Habitat for Humanity and for mediation of disputes among nations. And of course these are but a few examples.

Nor are the qualities of persistence and the ability to surmount setbacks important only for political figures. Bernard Marcus and

Arthur Blank, before cofounding The Home Depot and making a fortune, were fired from their jobs at the Daylin Corporation. They wrote, "The creation of The Home Depot began with two words in the spring of 1978: 'you're fired.'"[4] In 2001, the investment banking firm Sandler O'Neill employed 171 people. Eighty-three were in its World Trade Center office on the morning of September 11; 17 came out alive. Jimmy Dunne, the only surviving senior partner, led the effort to rebuild the firm. As he noted, "Sometimes it's easier when your back is against the wall. It was easy in that it was obvious as to what we had to do."[5]

In companies, particularly entrepreneurial companies, persistence and resilience are crucial for success. That's because it is almost invariably the case that products will need to be redesigned and strategies and tactics changed on the path to the market. Consider the case of Lars Dalgaard, the CEO of Success Factors. Dalgaard was a business unit leader at Unilever before graduating from the Sloan program at Stanford Business School in 1999. In 2001, he started Success Factors, a producer of human capital management software, and his first act was to buy the intellectual property of Austin Hayne. That company had a product, called the performance appraiser, that essentially automated and helped people with the performance appraisal process. After about seven years on the market, when Dalgaard purchased it, annual sales of this product were about $480,000. By 2006, Success Factors had 330 employees and was selling to major companies all over the world, had just raised $50 million in an oversubscribed round of venture capital funding, and had completed a quarter in which its sales were over $20 million. Now, don't get me wrong. In the meantime, Dalgaard had expanded the functionality of the product, had redesigned and reengineered it so it could scale on an application service provider model, and had also added other modules that did human resource functions besides appraisals. But essentially the foundation of this successful enterprise was a product that had failed and been left for dead.

Success Factors now sells its products in part by using a telephone sales force and generates a lot of its business that way. But it took four tries to get it right. First, Dalgaard hired senior people who thought they knew how to do sales, and they failed. Then, Success Factors outsourced its telesales effort but found that, after a couple of trial customer calls, the experience was so bad that it was little wonder that the outsourcing firm was not successful. Then the company hired some very young people who had no training in telesales. Dalgaard discovered that they had the right energy but lacked the skill and knowledge to be successful. So, he put in a training program that included rehearsing sales techniques and calls with the team, debriefing them on what went right and wrong on actual calls, and how to refine their pitch. On the fourth try, telesales became a big success.

It's also the case that persistence is important for inspiring the work and commitment of others. People won't follow a leader who isn't willing to do the hard work and they will leave if that leader does not both show and inspire commitment to completing the journey. When I met Sanjay Chakrabarty, a serial entrepreneur, at an event in Singapore, one of the first things he talked about was the importance of persistence, a lesson he had learned from experiences early in his career. Chakrabarty founded a company called Fastech with two friends while he was still in college, but when they graduated to good jobs, the company sort of just faded away. Later on, he actually saw a Silicon Valley company doing essentially what he had envisioned for Fastech, and mused that he had probably quit too soon. Then, while working on his master's degree in industrial administration, he started Global Business Systems, a systems integration company. He sold his interest to his cofounders and an institutional buyer, again probably walking away a little early.

Most recently, Chakrabarty founded MobiApps, a company headquartered in Singapore that uses wireless communications for machine-to-machine applications such as tracking, monitoring, and managing industrial equipment and assets. The company, with over 200 employees, $13 million in revenues after only two years, and sales in 13 countries, has received venture funding from 3i and Intel Capital, among others. As a successful entrepreneur, Chakrabarty has come to deeply understand what it takes to be successful:

> The one thing I can guarantee you is regardless of what you felt at the starting point, in terms of the vision and plan you have, your actual execution will be different than what you thought. Now why persistence is important is because almost always it takes longer. While you may have seen the need for the product, the willingness to pay takes longer. So here I think being a bulldog, whether it is getting a product out, or getting a product to a particular customer, and satisfying that customer, is crucial. Taking it from that first customer to getting three customers, and then taking it from three customers to 100 customers. At each one of these steps, I feel more often than not the people who I have seen succeed are the people who are absolutely sharply focused on the next milestone and who do not give up.[6]

Chakrabarty also has come to believe, from personal experience, that great educational credentials often work against people because they come to believe that their intelligence and educational pedigree will be sufficient to open doors and get things done. Or they expect to be in a high enough position that their direct reports will handle the actual work. Instead, success often comes from practical, not academic, smarts. He sees this all the time in engineering: "I have seen in production engineering that the people who are the best at debugging circuit boards and figuring out what is wrong with a particular unit are not the people who have the best engineering degrees but are the people who are really, really good technicians and have come up through the line. Therefore, they have this willingness to get their hands dirty."

Resilience and the ability to make something out of nothing is particularly important for small companies. One study of 25 businesses operating in depressed regions of the United States found that some companies were great at making something out of nothing while others weren't. For instance, the billing manager of a small telecom start-up that wanted to offer a variety of calling plans but didn't have the resources to go out and hire programmers to build the necessary software infrastructure taught himself the programming skills. He then cobbled together a system that saved back-office costs and still allowed the company to offer tiered pricing. The basic difference between success and failure among the companies in the study came down to either accepting resource constraints and giving up, or seeing possibilities for creating resources where others didn't.[7]

In thinking about the qualities to look for in the people you hire, or for that matter in thinking about the qualities you want to most develop in yourself, it is undoubtedly wise to remember this philosophical nugget attributed to movie star, writer, and director Woody Allen: "Eighty percent of success is showing up."

CHAPTER 20

No More Excuses

IT NEVER CEASES TO AMAZE ME: people come from all over the world to executive programs at Stanford Business School and learn amazing things about managing people more effectively to build competitive advantage and building high-commitment, high-performance organizational cultures. And their response? "Loved what you told us about treating employees better to capture their discretionary effort. Promoting learning by building a culture that tolerates mistakes? Great idea! Fixing root causes of problems, in the process sometimes making things worse before they get much better—makes a lot of sense. Trouble is, we can't do it. The boss should have been here. Too much day-to-day stuff that takes precedence. It takes too long to make these changes. Wish we had the time, money, and the other resources to change the way we do things, but you know how it goes."

It's as if a requirement for entering the ranks of senior management today is the ability to make excuses for why it's impossible to do things that most people agree are important. David Russo, the former head of human resources at SAS Institute and at Peopleclick, told me that when he gives speeches about how to build employee loyalty and motivation, it rarely takes more than 20 minutes before someone raises a hand and begins to explain that whatever Russo's saying can't be done in his or her organization. As he says, why bother showing up to listen to what to do if you aren't going to do it?

Excuses are also rampant in the public sector. Rudy Crew, head of Florida's Miami–Dade County school system and the former chancellor of New York City's schools, tells the following story about an incident in New York. He visited a school that was not doing well to meet with the principal and discuss necessary changes. The principal told Crew that the school had done well in the past, and then took the Chancellor into the schoolyard and pointed to some nearby public housing towers. He complained that many of the students who came from those projects had trouble speaking English, and that some mothers came to PTA meetings in house slippers. In other words, the school was failing because the students were too difficult to teach and their parents weren't helping with their education. Crew dismissed the principal that day, noting that if he gave up on the students, they would give up on themselves and that even though the task of educating disadvantaged students was difficult, there could be no excuse for not giving it every effort. As Crew told me, he couldn't be paying principals to engage in preemptory surrender.

When companies allow excuses to impede efforts to change, they don't merely fail to improve. The organizations risk losing out to those who see challenges as obstacles to be surmounted by diligent effort. After all, customers are happy to switch to competitors that actually fix problems instead of making excuses about why things can't be improved.

Consider the University of California at San Francisco's Carol Franc Buck Breast Care Center. In 1997, Laura Esserman, an MD and MBA graduate from Stanford, became its director. She had a vision: a facility where a woman could arrive in the morning and, in one location and in one day, receive an examination, a mammogram (if needed), and a biopsy (should that be needed), and leave at the end of the day with a diagnosis and a treatment plan—bypassing the typical delays as people went from one specialist to another, often having to carry their own medical records with them. Although this new arrangement made complete sense for the patient and even for the quality of medical care—after all, coordination among medical specialists would be easier if they were colocated—the obstacles were enormous. Each medical specialty—radiology, surgery, pharmacology, and so forth—had its own department and its own budget, and this was UCSF, a large, state-governed bureaucracy burdened with budget and employment rules that seemed to preclude any change. Nonetheless, Esserman did not accept excuses as to why something that made so much sense could not be done. With persistence and political skill, she created a successful center that has drawn national attention and where patient visits have increased from 175 a month in 1997 to 1,300 by 2003.[1]

So how do leaders break through the excuses that seem so common in organizational life? The first and most basic principle is not to accept reasons for why things that need to be done can't be. Carl Spetzler, a founder and former CEO of the consulting firm Strategic Decisions Group, told me that when he was still at SRI International in the early 1970s, he made a presentation to Merrill Lynch for a product that would become their Cash Management Account. At that time, interest rates were still regulated, the discount brokerage business was just beginning, and the idea of having one account that linked a credit card, check writing, money market funds, and securities trading together was extremely novel.

After Spetzler's presentation, Donald Regan, the CEO at the time, went around the room and asked for comments. The head of operations noted that with the average securities commission at that time of over $100, the fact that it cost more than $10 to process a transaction was not a problem—but Merrill would go broke with that cost structure if it got into the business of processing credit card receipts and checks. The head of marketing noted that banks were among Merrill's most important customers, and by issuing its own credit cards and processing checks, the company would be going into competition with those banks. The corporate counsel noted the many state and federal regulations that this new product would run afoul of—this was, after all, before all the deregulation in the 1980s. And so it went around the room. Then Regan told his team that he had heard all of their issues, and they were all both accurate and important. But it was also important strategically for Merrill Lynch to be the first to come to market with this innovative product. So he would now go back around the room and let each person who had described a problem now describe how he and his and team might attack it. Of course, faced with the need to not just identify some issues but to also actually fix them, the executives were remarkably creative with proposed plans and solutions. Merrill Lynch was the first major brokerage to launch an integrated financial package like the Cash Management Account, and it gained enormous business and profits by doing so—mostly because its CEO would not accept excuses for why things that were important to business success couldn't be done.

The next thing to do in the process of getting people to go beyond reasons why important things won't work or can't be accomplished is to articulate a vision that can inspire the effort required to overcome seemingly impossible obstacles. To Laura Esserman, that involves keeping the patients in focus, because who can look a breast cancer patient in the eye and tell that woman that she has to "settle" for how things are currently being done? So Esserman invariably invites patients or their loved ones to dinners and even staff meetings to tell their stories, as a way of maintaining the emphasis on the quality of care and the compassion with which medical services are delivered.

For Rudy Crew, it is expending boundless energy in "giving voice" to the issue of urban education in America and being an advocate for the children who are left behind when and if it fails. One of the powerful metaphors Crew frequently uses in his public appearances is that urban education is America's hill to climb. And while it might be interesting—and people have built quite successful careers—describing the hill, measuring the hill, walking around the hill, taking pictures of the hill, and so forth, sooner or later, someone needs to actually climb the hill. It is simply unacceptable to leave children not reading at grade level, because if kids can't read, they can't learn other subjects. And failure in school consigns them to failure in life, including in many instances going to jail. Crew talks patiently and endlessly to meetings of administrators, teachers, parents, the business community, and school board members to explain what must be done to provide opportunities for the children and how the school system can tackle what looks like a set of insurmountable obstacles.

Crew has a final word of advice for overcoming excuses: lead by example. Near the end of his time in New York, Crew, to keep himself focused on the work of education as contrasted with the endless politics that so frequently bedevil it, visited a fourth-grade classroom. There he saw a boy struggling with his math assignment, erasing his work, trying again, and erasing once more. Crew spent time with the boy, encouraging him to not give up and telling him that with persistence, he would eventually succeed. "Keep at it, you'll get it," he said. When he went to leave the room, the little boy came up to him and asked him who he was. When Crew replied he was the chancellor of New York City's schools, the boy was impressed. As only a young child could, he then asked Crew if he was any good at his job. Crew replied, sometimes he felt like was doing a good job but there were other days that he wasn't so sure. The boy smiled and told him, "Just keep at it. You'll get it."

Similarly, although it takes time away from her administrative and research work, Laura Esserman continues to provide care to patients. It not only keeps her connected to what she is trying to do and lets her make a difference one person at a time on days when the administrative obstacles seem insurmountable, her personal involvement in patient care gives her credibility with others she is trying to influence to change how that care is organized and delivered.

As the saying goes, the definition of insanity is doing the same thing over and over again while expecting different results. Many organizations understand that they need to change, why they need to change, and even how and in what direction they need to change. But they have all the excuses in the world about why they can't really do things differently. Excuses, therefore, drag organizations toward failure and mediocrity—toward an insane pattern of behavior in which the same mistakes get made again and again. As a leader, your job is to counteract the tendency to let excuses substitute for action. Or don't, and you and your team can trade excuses about why your company failed.

Part IV

Measures of Success

Rethinking Organizational Strategy

CHAPTER 21

The Real Budget Crisis

Stop Rewarding Forecasting and Negotiating Instead of Real Performance

SO THERE I SAT at a board meeting at a human capital software company, listening to the CEO and the CFO review our business performance. Compared with last year, profits and cash flow were both down a little and worse than that, the growth rate in new orders was also declining. We had competitors who were once smaller in sales but were now larger, which meant, of course, that they were growing faster, although this fact was not discussed as part of the financial review. But hey, we were ahead of plan for both the quarter and the year, so break out the champagne—or more to the point, the bonus dollars for our senior executives.

Is this any way to run a company or to measure organizational performance? It shouldn't be, but the bad news is that various forms of the scenario I've just described are played out every day in scores of companies that have succumbed to the tyranny of the budget.

There are a few companies, such as Svenska Handelsbanken, the large Swedish bank, that have gone budgetless; and the Beyond Budgeting Round Table is helping more organizations, including

American Express and Charles Schwab, avoid the numerous problems with managing on the basis of budgets. But at most companies, meeting or exceeding budgeted targets figures heavily in decisions about whether or not to pay out bonuses to senior managers and other employees and how large those bonuses should be. Companies assess their subjective performance—"Are we doing well or poorly?"—against meeting budget targets. Executives responsible for subunits and business functions are likely to get fired if they continually miss their budgets. Decisions about how much to spend on marketing activities or new capital investments often depend on whether the company thinks it has some slack resources, and once again, performance compared to budget looms prominently in assessing the degree of slack.

Nor are budgets and their importance confined to the private, for-profit sector. Every academic department, hospital, social service agency, governmental organization, and other nonprofit I know has a budget and guides its activities to meet budget targets and constraints.

Budgets do more than carry weight in many, if not most, important decisions. Budget planning is an enormous task, taking lots of management time and analytic resources. According to Jeremy Hope and Robin Fraser in their book, *Beyond Budgeting*, Ford Motor Company estimated that it spent $1.2 billion annually on its planning and budgeting process. Another survey showed that budgeting consumed between 20 and 30 percent of senior executives' time, and a 1998 study found that the average company invested more than 25,000 person-days per billion dollars of revenue in the planning and review process.[1] David Larcker, a cost accounting professor at Stanford, told me that few companies avail themselves of the data collected during the budgeting and planning process to actually understand their business models and what really drives success, adding that the enormous amount of data produced by the now-typical enterprise resource planning and financial systems was mostly used for "doing budgeting and planning for purposes of control."

Unfortunately, all this expenditure of time and effort seldom produces anything of much use to anyone; in fact, it almost certainly encourages unproductive behavior. That's because of the way most budgets are set and the consequences for meeting or missing them. Budgets are largely determined through an internal process in which senior executives, knowing that their own evaluations and financial payouts will be based at least in part on meeting or exceeding budgetary goals, try to estimate what the organization is likely to be able to do and then negotiate these figures with their board or supervisors. Senior executives have every incentive to set targets they can meet or, even better, exceed, while their boards typically try to set more ambitious goals. This process essentially rewards forecasting ability—can we predict what we are going to be able to achieve?—and the ability to negotiate with one's bosses. However, unless your organization is in the forecasting or negotiating business, it is far from evident that either of these skills should be so highly rewarded.

Meanwhile, neither the executives who are pushing for achievable (read, "lower") targets nor the board or the boss pressing for higher ones typically base their figures on anything more substantively meaningful than what the company or unit achieved last year and what people hope or expect it to achieve this year.

Of course, rewarding executives or companies for making their budgets just encourages them to—surprise!—game the system. So, a client for whom I was doing a series of executive seminars requested that I bill right away for all of the talks that year, including those scheduled months in advance. That way, the client could book the expense in the first half-year budget, where apparently it had some slack. Don't get me wrong. I'm not complaining, but purchasing ahead of need based on budget vagaries commits the company's capital before it needs to be spent. Executives at Hewlett-Packard told me the company would purchase both materials and services in advance to smooth out and meet budgetary targets, and a director on the company's board told me she found this behavior not only acceptable but, in fact, desirable as part of the process of meeting earnings expectations. It is, of course, only a short step from purchasing needed products in advance to meet budgetary targets to shipping products to distributors—so-called channel stuffing—and other forms of financial shenanigans. Meanwhile, to meet quarterly earnings numbers companies frequently resort to discounting their product or service prices as the end of the quarter nears, a behavior that simply encourages purchasers to wait until the end of the quarter to place their orders and thus results in the erosion of profit margins even if the numbers are temporarily met.

And the reverse problem can also occur, when companies don't spend money they should for fear of missing the budget target. A company making a highly innovative medical product curtailed the hiring of new salespeople in order to meet its budgeted expense and earning targets. In the short run, of course, new hires cost money, since before these folks can generate revenue, they must first be trained and get up to speed. But by skimping on needed salespeople to meet short run budget goals, the company may have damaged its longer-term ability to more rapidly capture market share, and ultimately lost competitive position to other companies entering this expanding market.

Or take another example. When, some years ago, I visited the Saks Fifth Avenue store then located at Stanford Shopping Center, I noticed a paucity of salespeople. The store manager confided that corporate headquarters was unhappy with the store's profitability, and the only immediately controllable expense was the staffing level. Fewer staff, of course, meant poorer customer service, which meant even lower sales . . . the store eventually closed. This death spiral plays out in industries ranging from airlines to retail—efforts to meet budget targets sometimes result in decisions that make the customer experience so noxious that sales continue to fall, requiring even more rounds of cuts.

And pursuing short-term budget goals sometimes causes not just companies but public-sector entities to skimp on long-term investments—in the companies' case in research and development; in the communities' case, in roads and other physical infrastructure. Indeed, an enormous number of perverse decisions are forced by the need to meet budgets, which is why Jack Welch, former CEO of General Electric, has said, "The budget is the bane of corporate America."[2]

The problem with—and, therefore, the potential solution to—the budget mess is that budgetary targets are frequently completely arbitrary, the result of forecasts and negotiation. That means it is possible to hit the targets while losing market share, falling behind technologically, and even going broke; and possible to miss the targets for doing things that actually enhance the long-term value and viability of the enterprise.

The obvious, although all-too-infrequently embraced, solution is to use budgets as rough guidelines for planning and forecasting purposes, but to base assessments of executives, departments, and companies on indicators that more fully capture relative competitive performance. For example, is the company or division doing better than external competitors—is it growing faster, is it gaining, or losing, market share? To return to the example with which I began, who cares if you are meeting some financial targets if virtually every indicator suggests the company is losing ground to the competition? The real questions should be: Is the company doing better than its competition in bringing new products and services to the market? Is the company outperforming its competition in its ability to attract and retain both customers and employees? In other words, get the assessment of performance off of an internal focus on budgets—which encourages logrolling, negotiating, and horse-trading—and onto measures that capture how well the company or its various departments or divisions are doing compared to some set of externally derived, relevant comparisons and standards.

As for the allocation of internal financial resources, once again what seems to be required is some honest assessments and decisions that are taken to achieve specific, important objectives. If the customer experience is important for the long-term viability of the enterprise, ensure that enough resources go into the staff and facilities that serve customers to provide the desired level of customer service. If new product and new technology development are critical for future success, ensure that enough resources go into those activities that the future is not sacrificed to meeting some current budgetary goal.

By the way, the foregoing is not an excuse for simply throwing money at problems or being inefficient. Once again, companies can use external benchmarks to help ensure the efficiency of their operations. So, for instance, you can compare how much money and time it takes your organization to bring out a new product or service compared with your competition, or how much it costs you to attract and retain employees or to keep customers thrilled compared with the competition. And in addition to using external benchmarks, you can also embrace the logic of continuous improvement and compare performance against past periods to ensure that things are getting better.

The absence of rigid budget adherence is not the same as financial anarchy. What I'm suggesting is that more strategic thinking be applied around the issue of performance targets and budgets. Instead of spending lots of time in meetings where people weigh past performance against budgetary goals, try holding meetings in which the discussion focuses on recent product and customer successes and failures, what's been learned, and how the company can do things to be more effective in the future. Not only will such sessions be more productive, but executives might even want to attend and contribute.

CHAPTER 22

Shareholder Return
Is the Wrong Measure
of Performance

MOST SENIOR EXECUTIVES these days, and the boards of directors they report to, are likely to base their most important decisions—hiring additional staff, acquiring or divesting lines of business, entering new markets—on what they guess will be the effect of the particular decision on their company's stock price. As one indicator of the importance of stock price to business decisions, a 2005 survey of investor relations professionals found that some 30 percent were highly involved in corporate development and strategic planning activities and 26 percent were highly involved in the analysis and planning for acquisitions and divestitures.[1]

Not only are management decisions affected by anticipated financial market reactions, lots of real resources get devoted to hyping a company's stock. For companies with under $500 million in market capitalization, some 85 percent have official investor relations departments; overall, some 94 percent of companies have an IR department with an average annual budget of $743,000.[2] At quarterly earnings time, press releases are carefully constructed and conference calls are held with analysts to explain the company's performance, again with an eye on the effect on the stock price. Getting new analyst coverage, particularly with a positive recommendation, is seen as a triumph, and yet more hours are spent trying to set investor expectations so that the firm can meet—or better yet, slightly exceed—them.

A lot of executive time is spent on share price and investor relations issues. One survey of CEOs of fast-growth companies indicated that these leaders were spending 11 percent of their time on corporate governance and administration, which includes investor relations. To put this figure in perspective, this was as much time as the CEOs spent on operations and more time than they were spending on product development.[3] Nor is this preoccupation with investors confined to the United States, in part because the U.S. shareholder-oriented business culture is diffusing globally. A study of 79 CEOs in Japan found that leaders spent some 2 percent of their working time on investor relations. Though this does not sound like very much, it was more time than the CEOs spent on unions, employee training, and outsourcing issues *combined*. The authors also documented a profound change in time allocation, with Japanese CEOs placing a comparatively greater emphasis on shareholders and focusing less attention on employees than in the past.[4]

The reason for this share price fixation—and its attendant diverting of focus from customers and products and employees? Companies and their leaders are obsessed with pleasing the financial markets and delivering, over increasingly brief time periods, the holy grail of corporate performance: total shareholder return (TSR). This is true even if the companies don't need to raise money from the capital markets, so in theory their short-run stock price should not matter.

This obsession derives from the belief that TSR is a measure—and a more accurate one than traditional accounting measures such as profitability or return on assets or sales—of the quality of a company and its management. How do we know this? Because

TSR is the dependent variable—the thing to be explained—in many studies in the academic and more popular management press. Does human resource management add value, and more specifically, what aspects of human resource management are most important? Watson Wyatt, the human resources consulting firm, uses its Human Capital Index (HCI) to evaluate all human resource management practices by considering their statistical effect on TSR.[5] The first thing noted on the Web site of the Great Place to Work Institute (the organization that helps *Fortune* construct its annual workplace rankings) is the fact that companies scoring high in the rankings also deliver better shareholder returns than comparable indices. In the academic literature, research often uses "event studies"—a measure of whether the stock market return was above or below what would be expected by general market movements—to assess the effects of events ranging from appointment of a new CEO to unionization.

Let's for the moment hold aside the arguments that the pursuit of shareholder return has distorted corporate behavior by forcing a more short-term focus. This short-termism is a real problem, as demonstrated by the facts that the National Investor Relations Institute has written reports and conducted workshops on how to build a longer-term orientation inside companies, and that in one study 66 percent of IR professionals said that coping with the short-term perspective of the investment community was a very important goal.[6] For the moment let's even ignore the fact that running a company to please the analysts means, for the most part, running a company to satisfy the demands of relatively young individuals with little or no experience actually running anything or even with much detailed knowledge about the products and the customers in the industry they cover. And let's also ignore the fact that many people believe that companies are or should be responsible to multiple stakeholders including their communities, customers, debt holders, and employees—not just shareholders. Even ignoring these three issues, there's still one huge problem with the obsession with stock price: by the criteria by which measures of anything are conventionally evaluated, it is not at all clear that shareholder return measures up.

One important measurement criterion is *reliability*—if you measure the same thing repeatedly, the measures should be consistent over time. For instance, measures of anything, from the simple to the complex—say, adult height and weight, general intelligence, personality dimensions—would be meaningless unless they were relatively stable over time.[7] Widely varying measures of the same thing are presumably due to measurement error.

But what do we know about stock price? Shareholder returns are incredibly uncorrelated from one period to the next. For instance, Nvidia, the number-one semiconductor company for shareholder return in 2001, ranked dead last in 2002, according to a study by L.E.K. Consulting.[8] Nor is this absence of stability in total shareholder return even surprising, if you believe modern finance theory. According to the random walk–efficient markets theory, stock prices are inherently both unstable and uncorrelated over time. That's because all of the available information is incorporated into the stock price at a given moment of time, so previous movements of stock price (TSR) are unable to predict future movements. Moreover, over the short term, too many exogenous factors, ranging from investor sentiment to general industry trends, affect stock prices for them to provide much insight into the quality of a company's management.

Nor is stock price a particularly valid measure. *Validity* means that one measure of something, in this instance the quality of a company or its management, should be strongly related to other indicators of the same construct. But the evidence shows little such relationship. For instance, as Baruch Lev has documented, over the past twenty or so years, the relationship between stock price and various accounting measures of firm performance has weakened considerably.[9] He noted that over intervals up to a year in length, "earnings account for only 5 percent to 10 percent of

the variation in stock returns," and this result holds for both reported earnings and earnings surprises.[10] Lev's interpretation of
his findings that earnings don't predict variation in stock price
(and, by inference, total shareholder return) is that accounting
information such as earnings per share has become less useful as
an indicator of company performance and management quality.
But there is a plausible alternative interpretation for his findings:
stock price is increasingly dissociated from economic measures
of company performance such as earnings, changes in earnings,
and assets and liabilities because stock price, under the influence of speculative trading, has become an inaccurate measure
of company or management quality.

Consider the effects of "earnings management"—trying to meet
or exceed analyst expectations through various accounting maneu-
vers and at the same time guide analyst expectations to a level
where they can be met or exceeded—on stock price. There is good
empirical evidence that firms do try to manage both earnings and
expectations to meet or exceed analyst targets.[11] This turns out to
be rational behavior because meeting expectations matters, if you
are interested in shareholder return. One sophisticated study
found that firms meeting expectations received a higher value from
the stock market, even after controlling statistically for indicators
of the true underlying value of the firm.[12] Think about what this
means. TSR includes a component of management performance
that is essentially the ability to forecast earnings and schmooze
analysts. Although this may be a measure of some underlying corporate capability, I don't see how economically meaningful that
capability is.

Because stock price movements reflect *unanticipated changes*
in company prospects rather than real economic performance
such as earnings or return on assets, TSR is not closely related to
the quality of a company, its management, or its performance.
For instance, according to the *Value Line Investment Survey* edi-
tion of September 8, 2006, the one-year return to shareholders

of AMR, American Airlines' holding company, was 56.6 percent, more than twice the return to shareholders of Southwest Airlines, who obtained a return of 26.9 percent over the same period. I doubt if anyone actually believes that American and its management are twice as good as Southwest, the only airline to be profitable every year since 1971.

If shareholder return has prominent effects on companies, their senior leadership, and their decision making but is problematic in its influence, one would expect to see companies doing things to avoid being as strongly influenced by pressures to maximize short-run shareholder return. And that is precisely what one observes. Some companies have tried to get away from the earnings expectations game by not providing guidance. After Edward Lampert created Sears Holdings by combining Sears and Kmart, he wrote in a letter to shareholders that "substantial amounts of time spent on investor relations activities 'distract and detract from accomplishing our fundamental objective of creating value for all our holders.'" Sears then stopped providing monthly sales figures and financial forecasts, and stopped holding analyst briefings and conference calls.[13]

But perhaps the best way to avoid the short-term pressures of the public capital markets is to go private—and that is precisely what lots of companies are doing. Lehman Brothers reported some 42 transactions of greater than $400 million in which companies went private just between May 2003 and mid-August 2006. Goldman Sachs reported that leveraged buyout volumes doubled between the first half of 2005 and 2006, and that completed LBO transactions increased from $19 billion in 1995 to some $198 billion in 2005, a tenfold increase in ten years. Nor is this increase just a consequence of attempts to engage in financial engineering. Kevin Callaghan, a partner at Berkshire Partners, a $6.5 billion private equity firm, told me that companies were going private because of the hassle factor of being a public company and also because leaders felt they could accomplish significant, value-creating business transformations more effectively out of the public markets.

In addition to going private, companies that are interested in avoiding the shareholder return myopia could focus on measures other than TSR—things such as customer and employee retention, the ability to bring new products and services to market, and traditional accounting measures that assess the efficiency with which capital is used. In other words, focus on the qualities and processes that actually produce better business outcomes. The business outcomes will follow. Consider a golf analogy: you won't improve your game by focusing on "managing" your score. But make the effort to improve those things that affect golf drives— grip pressure, shoulder rotation, and weight shift—and the score will take care of itself. The exact same thing is true for companies. Leaders need to reliably measure the processes that produce competitive success and not obsess about a measure, the stock price, that seems to be neither particularly reliable nor valid.

CHAPTER 23

Dare to Be Different

AT A CONFERENCE OF SENIOR EXECUTIVES from the grocery store industry sponsored by a large food and pet food manufacturer, I listened to people talk about innovation in their industry: self-service checkout (having customers do more of the work); grouping food products in different arrangements on the shelves; new store décor, including better lighting and different flooring material; different ways of pricing to improve margins; and various advertising and promotion strategies. Yawn. Take an airplane flight. With very few exceptions, can you tell them apart? The absence of food, service, or such amenities as pillows seems to characterize almost all the airlines as they seek the lowest common denominator for the customer experience. Actually, commonality of experience is pretty much the same in other industries, too—banking, movie theater chains, and, come to think of it, business schools.[1]

And why should we expect anything different? After all, benchmarking what others do has become de rigueur as a management practice. Consulting firms make good money essentially by learning what successful companies are doing and transferring knowledge and ideas across the companies that are their clients. Some businesses, such as the Advisory Board and the human resources consulting firm Saratoga Institute, have made benchmarking the very foundation of the service they provide their clients. Meanwhile, most business publications tell *what* others do much more than *why* they do it, presumably because their readers are interested in learning—and following—the practices of others.

There are some problems with all this copying, however. First, if companies are going to just imitate others, do we really need to pay CEOs such high salaries? I mean, how difficult should it be to hire some professionals to tell you what your competitors are doing and then do the same thing?

Second, and possibly even more importantly, it is virtually impossible to earn exceptional returns—and those returns could be exceptionally bad as well as exceptionally good, of course—by doing what everyone else does. If your company does what everyone else does, you will basically get the same results, plus or minus your skill at execution. You cannot benchmark your way to the top. Great companies are those that are able to see the inherent truth and value in a business model that breaks the mold in their industry. They also have the courage to act on their insight about how to do things differently.

Consider three examples. Conventional wisdom in the airline industry is that air service is a commodity and people will not pay for a superior customer experience. Consequently, telephone service is bad to nonexistent, check-in lines are long, and most companies seem to specialize in cutting every possible cost and frill—for instance, Northwest recently took out all movies on its domestic U.S. flights. In contrast, Singapore Airlines and Virgin Atlantic have had the courage to do things differently and have pursued a different approach for years. Singapore Airlines is justly famous for its outstanding customer service and for trying to provide *more* to its customers. The company was horrified—literally horrified—when British Airways introduced a better first-class "bed," vowing to catch up and surpass the BA experience. Virgin Atlantic Airways, which is now owned partly by Singapore Airlines, also adopted from its inception a policy of doing and providing more—for instance, having a business-class service comparable to first class on other airlines, providing a business-class experience for a premium economy price, and introducing sophisticated video systems in seatbacks in economy long before the company's competitors did so.

The business results speak for themselves. Virgin has been profitable from the first, and Singapore is about the only airline in the world, other than Southwest, that has been consistently profitable over the last several decades. That's because it turns out conventional wisdom is wrong. People actually *will* pay more if they get more. For instance, in the fall of 2006 I priced some routes in both business class and coach. For San Francisco to London, United's price was $463 for coach and $4,766 for business class. Virgin's prices for the identical dates and routes were $483 for coach (after all, coach is coach) but $6,932 for business class. From San Francisco to Singapore, United's coach fare was $1,094 and its business class fare was $2,902. The comparable fares on Singapore Airlines were $1,395 for coach and $4,123 for business class. As you can see, Singapore Airlines is able to get about a 30 percent price premium—same route, same day, same type of airplane— over United Airlines. Air service is not a commodity unless you treat it as such.[2]

Men's Wearhouse retails tailored men's clothing as well as shoes and casual wear, and now accounts for more than one out of five suits sold in the United States. It competes in what is a declining industry, because men don't dress up as much as they once did, but nonetheless has enjoyed an enviable record of growth in sales and earnings since it went public in 1992. The company's simple, commonsense, but seldom-copied insight? That businesses make money only when they sell their merchandise, not when they buy it. Therefore, unlike the typical retailer where the power is all in the hands of the buyers or the merchandisers—and thus the talented people avoid the neglected store operations unit at all costs—Men's Wearhouse strongly emphasizes the sales floor. The company invests extensively in training its wardrobe consultants in sales skills as well as product knowledge, sending them to four days at Suits University. It spends a lot of time thinking about how to tailor the shopping experience to its target audience—men—for instance by offering everyday low pricing instead lots of sales and promotions, and locating its stores in smaller malls so men don't have to wander through a large shopping center to get to the store. The emphasis on store operations and sales seems obvious, but few of the company's competitors have figured out their importance and adjusted their operations accordingly.

And then consider Whole Foods Market, the enormously successful retailer of natural and organic foods. Conventional wisdom in the grocery store industry seems to be that the only way to compete with Wal-Mart is to engage in endless cost cutting. Such cost cutting requires two things. To cut product costs, buy product by the railroad carload to obtain quantity discounts. This results in lower costs but also the same product assortment in every store. Second, to cut labor costs, keep staff numbers low and ensure that staff are as undereducated and untrained as possible so you don't have to pay them too much. That's why, when I ask people at other chains where to find items, I often get a blank stare. And forget about asking anyone in a typical grocery store a question about the products themselves.

Whole Foods' CEO John Mackey has figured out that people will, in fact, pay more for food that they actually want to eat. Since customer tastes can and often do differ by locale, departments such as fish, meat, cheese, and bakery in each store can select the merchandise best suited to local preferences. This practice gives up some economies of scale in purchasing but compensates by providing a tailored assortment of merchandise that is adjusted to consumer preferences on an ongoing basis. Furthermore, by having both more and better-trained people in the stores, the customer service experience is enhanced; the staff can actually answer questions about health and beauty aids or about organic produce and antibiotic-free fish and meat—and help sell the merchandise.

So why don't more companies figure out the basics of their business and implement these insights in their operations? One big barrier to breaking away from the crowd is that many companies believe that their performance is highly constrained by the structure of their industry—that they can't really do much better than what industry conditions permit. But this idea is clearly wrong. In 2002, on the occasion of *Money* magazine's 30th anniversary, the magazine published a list of the best-performing stocks over the time of its existence.[3] Number one was Southwest Airlines, with a compounded annual return of about 26 percent. Also in the top five were Wal-Mart and Walgreens, companies that operated in the ferociously competitive retail industry. Kansas City Southern, a railroad, was also among the top five best performing stocks. These companies compete in what most people, including strategy guru Michael Porter, would think are doomed industries having none of the characteristics that, according to his "five forces" model, would predict strategic success: barriers to entry, threat of substitutes, limited rivalry, and market power with respect to either customers or suppliers.[4] The airline industry has been beset with bankruptcies; retailing is also littered with the carcasses of failed companies, some of them former giants. The evidence from studies by strategy consulting firms is clear: you are much better off being a well-run company in a lousy industry than being a poorly run company in an industry that seems to offer unlimited opportunity. And being well run entails, first and foremost, seeing the obvious customer needs and preferences and meeting them.

Meeting customer needs requires having the wisdom and courage to do things that, at first glance, seem not to make sense in the short term. Les Schwab Tire Centers, the billion-dollar privately owned tire and auto repair chain located mostly in the Pacific Northwest, will fix flat tires for free and will send someone to your house to change a tire occasionally. If you pull into one of its facilities, service personnel literally run to greet you—none of the waiting in line that you find in many dealerships. And the waiting rooms hardly look as if they belong in an automobile repair facility; they are clean, attractive, and offer free coffee. All of this costs money—the nicer facilities, the free services, the staffing levels that permit customers to get in and out of the stores quickly. But by offering an outstanding level of customer service and creating a service experience that is not what one would expect in the auto repair industry, the company has been able to attract a fanatically loyal customer following that has, for instance, given it about a 70 percent market share in the Portland, Oregon, replacement tire market—this in an industry, that, like airlines and retail, is characterized by fierce competition and few barriers to entry.

Lots of companies have the essential insights—or at least the front-line employees do—about what would make the product or service experience better. But caught up in the follow-the-leader, benchmarking game, companies often don't have the courage to act on this knowledge. And when they do, investment analysts and boards of directors get nervous, because the question always arises, "Why are you doing something different?" The best answer to that question, in my view is, "We are different because we want to be better." There is no guarantee of success, but it is clear that simply following the crowd won't create a truly outstanding organization.

CHAPTER 24

Curbing the Urge to Merge

SO OFF I GO TO MACY'S to buy some sheets that have been advertised. Plotting carefully to be there when there is some remote chance I can get waited on, I arrive at 8:30 on a weeknight, expecting the store to be nearly empty. It is, but the absence of any customers other than me is insufficient to induce any of the three salespeople, busily talking among themselves, to wait on me. I am soon at Bed Bath & Beyond, where I am greeted at the door and receive all the help I need. In the many media discussions about what plagues department stores in general, and Macy's in particular, I hear lots of talk about Wal-Mart, Target, and other discount competitors but almost no mention of the operational problems that make service virtually nonexistent. And what is Macy's solution to its competitive challenges? Purchase the May Company—and change the names of all the subsidiary chains to Macy's!

Macy's—or more properly, Federated Department Stores—is not the only company seeking salvation from execution failures though a merger. I was on the board of a $200 million manufacturer of tamper-evident plastic bottle caps and bottles for the dairy, water, and juice industry. Faced with consolidation among its buyers and a consequent squeeze on margins, the company could have driven its costs down—it had a market-leading position—and innovated in its products and services to keep its existing customers happy. But no—it decided to embark on a $36 million acquisition of a packaging company selling into different industries, using different technologies, and located in a different part of the country. The purchase destroyed a lot of shareholder value, reducing the value of the company's equity by more than 50 percent.

Nor is the merger instinct confined to old-line industries—technology companies succumb as well. A human capital software company selling a hosted employee selection application that was focused on the hourly workforce needed to expand its offering to include selection for salaried employees and applicant tracking. It could have developed those capabilities in-house. But the board was told that this choice was too slow, risky, and costly. So, two mergers and many millions of dollars and millions of issued shares later, where was the company? The promised functionality sought through the mergers was more than 18 months late—probably longer than it would have taken to the develop the software in-house—and the software was basically being redesigned and integrated by the same people who didn't get to build it from scratch in the first place.

The list of failed mergers could fill this book, and several more. The evidence clearly shows that many, albeit not all, mergers are failures—not delivering their intended financial or operational benefits and, in the process, destroying shareholder value.[1] Some estimates are that as many as 70 percent of all mergers are bad for the acquiring company.[2]

When companies face competitive challenges and business difficulties, they can do one of two things: directly address and fix the problems, or try to remedy their difficulties through financial engineering such as mergers, which are often undertaken in an effort to "buy" growth. The merger strategy also has the side benefit of diverting attention from the company's management problems and operational weaknesses by absorbing boards of directors and senior leadership in the details of the "deal." Some senior employees and observers of Hewlett-Packard believed that its merger with Compaq was an effort by its CEO, Carly Fiorina, to divert attention from the company's failure to meet its quarterly goals. Although using mergers to try and remedy business difficulties may be both risky and foolish—I mean, you would undoubtedly run from a doctor who prescribed a remedy that failed most of the time—it is nevertheless the remedy that is often preferred. And that's why the effective leadership of companies entails curbing the urge to merge.

The data and the many anecdotes in the press about merger difficulties—think AOL-Time Warner, Daimler-Chrysler, Ford-Jaguar, and Wells Fargo-First Interstate Bank is a very partial list—beg two questions: Why do people opt for mergers in the first place? and Why is failure such a common outcome?

The answer to the first question is, in part, that bane of corporate performance—executive ego. The self-enhancement bias suggests that almost everyone believes that she or he is more intelligent and effective than average.[3] This overly optimistic view of our abilities is, of course, going to be worse for CEOs—after all, they generally *are* way above average, which is how they got to their positions in the first place. So, executives believe that even though most mergers between technology companies don't work, the one they are proposing will. Even though most mergers of comparably sized companies are disasters, the CEO and senior team's consummate skill in merger integration and incorporating new employees will ensure that everything turns out all right. Of course, it seldom turns out that way. And interestingly enough, a study by business school professors Matthew Hayward and Donald Hambrick found that the greater the hubris and overconfidence of the chief executive, the more the company that person leads tends to overpay for acquisitions.[4] The aphorism, "Pride goeth before a fall," seems to empirically hold true when it comes to mergers.

The second reason why companies pursue mergers is that they are exciting. Mergers involve investment bankers, whose fees depend on doing deals. And the bankers are great at selling deals—if they weren't, they wouldn't be in the business very long. Investment bankers are smart and fun to talk to. And if the merger gets done, there is a nice closing dinner and those lovely pieces of plexiglass. It is intellectually exciting to think about the alternative partners that might help a company increase its growth or build out its product more quickly. How much more mundane and unexciting are the tasks of actually hiring more employees, motivating the ones you've got, figuring out what customers really want, and delivering it to them. Mergers often seem like a faster solution to problems than solving those problems internally. Mergers also often seem less risky than trying to solve the problems internally. Admitting that you have execution problems is tantamount to admitting there were management miscues. Better to focus on external forces and external solutions—and after all, all those people who are going to earn fees from the deal keep blowing in management's ear about the risks of trying to build growth or product inside the company when the answer is just sitting there for the negotiation. Execution and operational excellence is hard work, but more than that, it is often not very glamorous. Mergers have sex appeal. No wonder the urge to merge.

Plus which, in a world in which everyone else is doing deals, who wants to be left out? Yes, corporate leaders succumb to conformity pressures just like kids in the schoolyard. Mergers get attention from analysts and sometimes from the media, and the ego-driven CEO likes that attention. And the idea that everyone else is doing it truly provides "cover" or rationale for merging. After all, can everyone else be wrong? (The answer to that question, based on evidence, is no, everyone can't be wrong, but a vast majority of them might be.) And then there is the related rationale—since everyone else is merging and consolidation is going on in our industry, we'll be left out—sort of like the game of musical chairs. But it is far from clear that this a valid rationale, given the nonexistent relationship between size and profitability in most industries.[5] But the psychological principle of scarcity comes into play—we want things that are scarce or might be scarce—so if possible merger partners are disappearing, companies are influenced to move before they miss out on the action.

And why do mergers fail so often? Having seen mergers proposed and, thankfully, turned down, and having participated in or observed some failed mergers at close range, I think I can shed some light on this question. First, failure is a common outcome of the merger process because of the operation of "self-delusion" during the negotiation and due diligence process—we see what we want to and expect to see. CEOs don't embark on a merger without expecting to conclude the deal, in most instances. Therefore, because of the process of escalating commitment: the more time, energy, and resources that get invested in the negotiation and due diligence process—the harder it is to walk away. And because of the essential overconfidence that so frequently bedevils companies and their leaders, the healthy skepticism that ought to guide purchases of anything is largely missing.

Second, it is actually almost impossible to do due diligence to the extent necessary to uncover problems, even if companies and their leaders wanted to—which they mostly don't. That's because the problem of truth telling, which occurs in companies anyway because people don't like to be bearers of bad news or negative information, gets magnified in a merger situation. If the target company and its managers and employees are, as is typically the case, going to be financially better off if the merger goes through than if it doesn't, why would anyone expect people in the company being acquired to be forthcoming about the weaknesses and business issues that may characterize that company? And holding this aside, due diligence, even if it is extensive, will almost never uncover the tacit, unwritten issues and problems that require time and close observation to really understand.

And the third reason that mergers often don't work is that the very process itself can create turmoil and uncertainty. Employees leave because they are worried about their future. After the merger is completed, employees of the acquired company may leave if the deal has left them so financially comfortable that they can afford to retire or take time off. Competitors use the fact that, in the case of the target company, it will disappear and in the case of the acquirer, that it will be distracted, to dislodge customers. This is precisely the position taken by Dell during the Hewlett-Packard–Compaq merger, and by SAP trying to steal a march while Oracle acquired PeopleSoft. The negotiation itself, over deal terms that can easily run 80 pages—in a "simple" transaction—diverts senior management attention from the day-to-day activities of running the business. The merger process obviously takes time and attention, and time and attention focused on the merger obviously can not be focused on customers, products and services, and employees.

So here are some suggestions about how to avoid these common merger problems. First, follow the adage from medicine and forgive and remember. Do something unusual—go back and actually revisit past merger decisions, admit when they turned out badly, figure out why, and learn so you and your colleagues don't keep making the same mistakes over and over.

Second, beware of too much management consensus in the boardroom. When Alfred Sloan ran General Motors, if he couldn't find opposition to a decision, he'd postpone it, figuring a lack of dissent meant that the decision had not been considered carefully enough. Everything has a downside, after all, and even the best decisions have risks and costs. Find and even encourage people to surface dissenting views. As my colleague Bob Sutton is fond of saying, if two people agree all the time, one of them is redundant.

The urge to merge remains an addiction in too many companies. Doing deals seems much more fun and intellectually interesting than fixing fundamental operational issues. So, maybe the best advice is similar to what is useful in dealing with any other addiction or temptation: just say "no."

CHAPTER 25

Don't Believe the Hype About Strategy

THERE I SAT at yet another board meeting, listening to the chief executive drone on about sales strategy and product strategy as he pointed to slick slideware filled with analyses of potential markets and buzzwords about our competitive positioning in the design visualization software market. Then it dawned on me—almost no one in the room, including the person talking, had actually visited a customer or, for that matter, even used the company's product in their own work. Unable to contain myself, I blurted out, "How about this for a sales strategy? Instead of sitting around talking about customers, why not call on some? Why not try to sell to them and, at the same time, find out what they like and don't like about our product so we can improve it?" I was, of course, politely ignored, and the meeting continued.

This scene, or something like it, is repeated way too frequently these days, inside far too many organizations, and it captures a lot about what is wrong with "strategy" as it has come to be defined and practiced in business. First of all, there is often much too much emphasis on the quality of the presentation and the pitch rather than the quality and business acumen of the ideas.

Several former Stanford MBA students have described quitting leading consulting firms in disgust because they could simply not get excited about worrying about what template, colors, and fonts to use for client presentations and found obsessing over the specific order of materials in the "deck" (consulting jargon for the PowerPoint slides) instead of actually dealing with substantive business issues to be a waste of their time. The idea of banning PowerPoint presentations from meetings makes more sense to me all the time. Former U.S. Joint Chiefs of Staff chairman General Henry Shelton and Scott McNealy, the cofounder and former CEO of Sun Microsystems, are among those that have banned the use of PowerPoint in meetings.[1] Long presentations take up too much time and often divert attention from the real issues. As Edward Tufte, Yale emeritus professor of political science, computer science, and statistics, has written, typical PowerPoint presentations "elevate format over content," turn everything into a sales pitch, and essentially let the speaker dominate the meeting, thereby limiting the interchange of ideas so essential for creative thinking.[2] I have come to believe, having seen more than a few presentations from consultants and investment bankers myself, that the fancier the presentation, the less the content.

Second, there is often a lot of emphasis on talk—on sounding smart—in the strategy formulation process and a lot of time spent sitting around thinking and planning instead of going out and trying some stuff, seeing what works, and learning by doing. That's because strategy—trying to figure out *what* to do—is intellectually interesting and challenging and, as a consequence, more intriguing to senior leaders and the smart people who populate consulting companies. After all, you can use game theory to try and figure out competitive responses and feel smart in the process. And you can throw around all those buzzwords you learned in business school: first-mover advantage, multipoint competition, value chain analysis, hypercompetition—the list goes on and on.

You can dazzle your colleagues with your intellect and sophistication, and that is often what is required for success in companies—seeming smart, rather than doing smart things.[3]

No wonder that a survey conducted by the National Association of Corporate Directors found that CEOs ranked strategic planning as second in importance to their companies.[4] Yet in spite of all the emphasis on strategy at the board and senior executive level, there is precious little evidence that it really is a source of success. The research on the effects of strategic planning generally finds it has no effect on corporate performance. Meanwhile, planning exercises absorb enormous amounts of resources and sometimes divert attention from pressing implementation issues.[5]

In order to achieve sustainable competitive advantage—another term from the strategy literature—you must be able to do something that your competitors cannot readily imitate or duplicate. And strategy *content* is both easily discerned and imitated. Companies announce their strategies in their public filings and annual reports as well as in their analyst conference calls and company presentations. Public companies—through their financial results—disclose their costs at least in general terms and also report how well their strategies are working. And if that were not enough, you can always hire one of those ubiquitous strategy consulting firms to research anything else you need to know about what a company's strategy is, how well it is working, and how you can imitate or attempt to counteract it.

Moreover, most successful strategies are deceptively simple. SAS Institute—the largest privately owned software company in the world with annual sales of over $1.5 billion in 2005—eschews much formal strategic planning. Instead the company tries to follow this simple strategy, told to me by its cofounder, John Sall: "Listen to your customers, listen to your employees, do what they tell you." Southwest Airlines' strategy involves increasing its aircraft utilization through quick turnarounds and enhancing the customer experience by flying on time and getting people and their bags to the same place at the same time. Simple strategies turn out, somewhat paradoxically, to be a big barrier to imitation. As Greg Brenneman, the chief operating officer who helped CEO Gordon Bethune lead the turnaround at Continental Airlines in the 1990s, noted, people have many ways of saying that if things were that simple, they would have already thought of and done it.

What is extremely difficult to copy—and what therefore does provide competitive advantage—is the *way* a company implements and executes its strategy. Anyone can talk about being the technology leader or providing outstanding customer service. But few organizations can actually make good on that promise. That's why Wells Fargo CEO Richard Kovacevich once said he could leave the company's strategic plan on a plane and it wouldn't make any difference: "Our success has nothing to do with planning. It has to do with execution."[6]

The other problem with today's overemphasis on strategy is the tendency to build in various forms of rigidity. Strategy, after all, is designed to tell a company not only what to do but also what not to do—what customers and products and industry segments to avoid, either because they don't play to the company's strengths or aren't economically attractive, or some combination of the two. But markets and customers don't really care about a company's strategy or even its strengths and weaknesses.

In the early 1980s, David Kearns, then CEO of the Xerox Corporation, described how the company had gotten into trouble by ignoring Japanese competitors such as Canon and Ricoh. Their small copiers were not considered to be comparable to Xerox's larger machines, they sold them not by the "click" or copy, as Xerox did, but as capital purchases, and they sold them to other buyers than the reprographics departments that bought the Xerox machines. While Xerox ignored the small copiers—just as IBM at first ignored the personal computer as not being within its market space—the competition stole a march on an important, rapidly growing, emerging market segment. The comment "It's not in our business" or "our strategy" begs the question of whether it *ought* to be.

There are ways around this rigidity, but they involve listening to customers and the market and being adaptable—including being willing to build new skills and competencies, and not sticking with some strategy just because it is the strategy. Consider IDEO, one of the most successful product design companies in the world, which has designed Nike sunglasses, the Apple mouse, television sets, medical equipment, and even the mechanical whale for the movie *Free Willy*. IDEO's mantra is that "enlightened trial and error outperforms the planning of flawless intellects," a philosophy it applies not just to the design of its products but also to itself, its organization, and how it conducts business. It has built an experimenting, do-what-it-takes culture. IDEO had made a good living by designing products for the high technology industry. But during the technology crash in 2001, it needed to reinvent itself, and it did. The company began designing products for consumer goods companies like Procter & Gamble. And it even got into the business of designing experiences, which helped it garner business figuring out how to design hospital emergency rooms, for instance, to make things less confusing and fearful for patients.

So, instead of sitting in meetings and spending time preparing fancy PowerPoint presentations, develop your strategy adaptively, by using your company's best thinking at the time, learning from experience, and then trying again, using what you have learned. Building an experimenting, mistake-forgiving, adaptive culture provides a competitive advantage that lasts, because that sort of environment is much more difficult to copy than some dogmatic strategy. Under almost all circumstances, fast learners are going to outperform even the most brilliant strategists who can't adapt.

Part V

Facing the Nation

Organizations and Public Policy

CHAPTER 26

In Praise of Organized Labor

What Unions Really Do

IF THERE'S ONE WORD that never fails to raise the blood pressure of my friends in business, particularly in the United States but internationally as well, that word is *unions*. In many people's minds, organized labor is the archenemy of the basic prerequisites for economic success—flexibility, efficiency, and a relentless emphasis on business results. Even presumably progressive thinkers and executives in countries with a strong union tradition see unions as anachronisms in the modern world. Of course, people will sometimes admit that organized labor may have been important and useful in earlier, less enlightened times and acknowledge the role of labor organizations in promoting workplace safety, outlawing child labor, and limiting working hours. However, with these reforms now thoroughly institutionalized in both law and custom, the advocacy role of unions seems less valuable. Today, many leaders believe that "management gets the union it deserves." The implication is that good, progressive human resource management practices both forestall unionization and also make union representation unnecessary to ensure sound people management practices.

Like much conventional wisdom, however, the prevailing views about unions are often inaccurate or incomplete. So, it's useful to set the record straight so that organizations and their leaders can make better and more profitable decisions.

Consider first the effect of unions on wages. Yes, there is evidence that unions raise wages—that is, after all, their primary reason for existence.[1] But higher wages do not automatically translate into either lower profits or diminished competitiveness. Most evidence suggests that labor unions negatively affect company profits primarily when companies enjoy either a monopoly position or substantial market power.[2] In other words, when companies are able to extract monopoly rents, unionization ensures that some of those rents get shared with the workforce and not just the owners, but in competitive market positions, there is essentially little or no union effect on company profitability.

The phenomenon of indirect and feedback effects looms large in understanding how wages can go up without profits going down. First, higher wages will attract more skilled employees—labor markets are no different in that regard than other markets, and it is often the case that you get what you pay for. Firms compete for labor. Unionized firms, generally offering higher wages and working conditions that are more attractive on other dimensions as well, pull in more skilled and educated people. Such employees are able to accomplish more per unit of time they work, and thus are more productive. So, the higher wage effect does not necessarily translate into higher costs.

Second, higher wages decrease turnover—multiple studies in both unionized and nonunion settings demonstrate the negative relationship between relative wages and quit rates. Turnover is expensive, not only in terms of the direct costs of replacing those who leave but also in the loss of experience, skills, and tacit knowledge. So, curbing turnover produces benefits for the company. Third, higher wages, just like higher prices for anything, encourage companies to economize on the use of labor. In the case of the price of employees, that means investing in capital equipment, investing in additional training, and ensuring that work methods are as efficient as possible so that labor hours and their associated costs don't get wasted. These consequences—all of which enhance labor productivity—are why studies in a number of industries, such as construction, demonstrate that unionized workforces are actually more productive than their nonunion counterparts.[3] In many cases, the productivity advantages that come from a more highly skilled, experienced, and effectively deployed workforce with more capital equipment completely outweigh the extra wage costs, leaving total costs unaffected and productivity actually higher in the unionized settings.

Unions not only affect the level of wages, they also affect the distribution of earnings. Unions have an egalitarian ethos—necessary to effectively organize for collective action—and therefore generally strive for a more equal wage structure. To the extent unions are able to achieve their aims, therefore, unionization is associated with less inequality in wages.[4] Although there is much discussion about how differentiated wages helps organizational performance by permitting a strong pay for performance ethos, the available evidence suggests that this is seldom the case. In settings ranging from baseball teams to university faculty to top management teams, the consistent finding is that more variation in wages is negatively associated with various performance measures.[5]

Furthermore, this greater level of equality manifests itself in diminished wage discrimination against less favored segments of the labor force. So, there is evidence that unionization is associated with smaller differences in wages between whites and minorities, between men and women, and less wage inequality more generally.[6] The positive effects of unions on reducing these wage differentials are not generally well known, nor are they frequently discussed.

The increasing wage inequality in the United States—where the gap in income between the highest and lowest deciles or quintiles has widened considerably—and in other countries has many causes. But certainly one contributing factor has been the decline in unionization. Some social observers see this increasing inequality as a problem, potentially leading to political instability and alienation of those segments of the workforce that have not benefited from increasing wealth. To the extent that wage inequality is a problem, unionization provides a part of the solution through its effect on the distribution of earnings.

There is currently a lot of discussion about the implementation of a "high road" competitive strategy in which advanced industrialized countries stop trying to compete on the basis of labor costs—a battle they can never win—but instead compete on the basis of innovation, productivity, and brainpower. In this effort, the evidence suggests that the implementation of high-performance work practices is useful. So, another issue is how unionization affects the implementation of the best human resource management approaches.

Contrary to what many believe, having a unionized workforce is not antithetical to the implementation of so-called high-commitment or high-performance work practices—things such as investment in training, working in self-managed teams, longer-term time horizons for the employment relationship (read, more job security), information sharing, and so forth. Rather, the empirical evidence suggests that unionization is positively associated with the implementation of such practices and in fact may make changing to a "high road" management approach more likely and easier.[7] At worst, unions have no effect on the implementation of these practices; there is almost no evidence that suggests they have a negative effect.

Furthermore, research suggests that many high-commitment work arrangements are actually relatively fragile. That's because the typical response to almost any sort of economic stress or competitive stringency is to abandon strategies that entail investing in people or social capital more generally. Training expenditures are among the first budget items cut, and companies resort to layoffs at the first sign of economic stress, even though the evidence is that layoffs are often counterproductive. Thus, ironically, unionization may actually lead to higher persistence of high-commitment work arrangements because unions act as a countervailing force to short-term pressures to abandon such arrangements.

In some instances, the implementation of aspects of high-performance work arrangements may actually be enshrined in the contractual language jointly negotiated between companies and their unions. During the 1980s, Donald Petersen, then CEO of Ford Motor Company, implemented total quality management and transformed Ford's culture, with dramatic business results. He credits his ability to persevere with the change program, even through setbacks and reversals, to the presence of the United Auto Workers Union and the fact that aspects of the change were embedded in the formal contract. In a similar fashion, people at Saturn, at one point a model not only of union-management cooperation but a high-productivity producer of high-quality cars, credited its contract with the UAW with helping to maintain cooperative, high-performance work practices.

But it is perhaps in medicine where the positive effects of unionization can most clearly be seen. The relationship between personnel practices and practical outcomes is straightforward in health care: when care is bad, patients die or get sicker. And the factors producing better or worse patient outcomes are pretty well known.

Studies summarized by a report from the Institute of Medicine show that lowering the nurse-patient ratio—a short-term cost-cutting tactic embraced by many hospital administrators and political figures but vigorously opposed by nurses' unions—is associated with higher rates of patient infection, pneumonia, cardiac arrest, and death.[8] In California, nurses and their labor organizations lobbied for a law to mandate more nurses per patient. Once the law was passed, these same organizations fought attempts by health care organizations and governor Arnold Schwarzenegger to delay its implementation. Although pejoratively called "special interests" by some companies and politicians, it is unclear why labor organizations and the employees they represent are any more "special interests" than the for-profit health care and hospital organizations that were their opponents. In any event, by bringing public attention to the clear and well-established relationship between staffing ratios and patient outcomes, nurses' organizations were instrumental in preserving practices that the evidence shows produce better patient care.

And there are other effects of collective bargaining that are particularly important in affecting health care outcomes. The process often institutionalizes and to some extent compels more power sharing and communication between administrators and front-line staff. Front-line health care employees not only have the most direct impact on patient outcomes but also have the knowledge about what works and what doesn't, so listening to them makes good sense. For instance, a 2004 study of the risk-adjusted death rates from heart attacks in 344 acute-care hospitals in California found that facilities with unionized nurses had a 5.5 percent lower mortality rate than non-union hospitals. These results held after controlling statistically for many other factors that might be associated with unionization. The authors concluded that it was probably the increased power the unionization provided to nurses as well as the increased level of joint decision making that led to the better patient care results. That same study found that much of the gain disappears when union-management relations are adversarial.[9]

The Kaiser-Permanente Medical Group, a $28 billion U.S. health maintenance organization, has been a pioneer in partnering with its various labor unions in an effort to produce better health and productivity outcomes by involving its employees in joint decision making. In 1997, following some years of adversarial labor relations, including strikes, the organization launched a formal labor-management partnership with its 26 local unions.

The partnership implemented a joint decision-making model, where senior company officials and their union counterparts were expected to jointly consult on and jointly decide significant organizational personnel and policy decisions. Of course, shared decision making was not completely embraced by the physician leaders, a lot of training and many conferences notwithstanding, and the implementation of the partnership principles has been, not surprisingly, uneven. Nonetheless, in those regions and facilities where shared decision making and joint responsibility have taken hold, the results have been very good. Workplace injuries fell by more than 20 percent, employee satisfaction climbed from 65 percent in 2000 to 80 percent in 2003, and plan-member satisfaction increased by 3 percent. Although this latter number may seem small, many Kaiser members have little or no dealings with the organization from one year to the next—it is only those who get sick who have much contact. Thus, healthy members, the vast majority, won't change their assessment of Kaiser between surveys. In that context, a 3 percent increase in satisfaction, Kaiser officials maintain, is actually a very strong result. Most impressive of all, the cost savings attributed to the partnership arrangement now exceed $100 million.

Some of the most competitive and successful private-sector organizations are unionized. Southwest Airlines, the only carrier to have been profitable each of the past 35 years, is the most unionized of all U.S. airlines. UPS is unionized. So it is possible to be economically successful and have labor organizations at the same time.

It is even possible, in a world in which many companies fight labor organizations, to use cooperation as part of a strategy to achieve competitive advantage by being different. Consider Cingular Wireless, which remained neutral while 18,000 employees joined the Communication Workers of America. At the same time the company also achieved the best financial results in its history; and Lew Walker, the vice president of human resources, believes there is a connection between the two. That's because the company got "engaged employees who are focused on customer service and building the Cingular network rather than nursing grudges against management." Moreover, the CWA, because of its positive relations with Cingular in contrast to the battles it has fought with other telecommunications companies, actually "launched a campaign to market Cingular's service," thereby helping the company with its marketing.[10]

Labor organizations have a number of positive effects that are generally overlooked or not acknowledged. This is not to say that labor organizations are all completely honest and enlightened—by the way, neither all are managements, in case you have forgotten WorldCom, Tyco, Enron, and the rest. But the simple truth is that the lessons to be drawn from unionized health-care workers about the importance of information sharing, joint decision making and employee involvement, and the benefits of a more experienced and stable workforce apply to virtually all industries, and to non-union work environments as well. The advantage of collective bargaining is that the contractual arrangements make management backsliding on implementing high-performance management practices less likely.

CHAPTER 27

What to Do—and Not Do—About Executive Pay

NEARLY EVERY DAY, some commentator or another is weighing in on the issue of executive pay. There seem to be two complaints. First, executive pay, and particularly chief executive pay, is increasingly excessive. Think about it: in 2005, the average pay of CEOs of large companies was $10.5 million. Furthermore, CEO pay is an ever larger multiple of the pay of front-line employees; by one estimate, CEO pay was 36 times what an average worker earned in 1976, 131 times in 1993, and had ballooned to 369 times as much by 2005.[1] This ratio is much higher than that in other industrialized countries such as Japan, Spain, France, or even the United Kingdom. Moreover, the ratio of chief executive pay to the pay of even other executives has doubled since the 1960s.[2] The second complaint is that executive pay is not tied to "performance"—typically total return to shareholders as measured by changes in the stock price—so that executives can get rich even if their firms aren't doing that well and other shareholders aren't getting great returns.

Many people have suggested reforms, some of which have already been implemented. These reforms typically are of three types. The first entails changing the presumed "power structure" on the board of directors, such as having a nonexecutive chairperson of the board (something that was once rare but is now increasingly common), having compensation committees comprised solely of independent directors, and changing voting rules so that outside shareholders have more influence over the process by which directors are nominated and elected. The second approach focuses on changing the tax rules to constrain executive pay. A number of years ago the tax rules were amended to make pay over $1 million not deductible unless that pay was tied to performance. This change had virtually no effect, as all compensation committee statements in proxies lay out how the CEO pay determination process is related to performance. So, it is unlikely that there are very many—if any—companies subject to this particular reform.

The third type of reform, and the one that seems to get the most attention and advocacy, argues for more disclosure about the components of executive pay and how pay is set. First, companies were required to disclose various forms of incentive compensation such as stock options and bonuses, and compensation committees were required to provide details of their pay-setting philosophy and process. Now there are going to be even more stringent disclosure requirements—for example, details of deferred compensation such as retirement benefits and perquisites such as use of the corporate jet and company-paid apartments, both for active and retired executives.

Having participated on the compensation committees of both private and public company boards, and having read the relatively large empirical literature on executive pay, I am struck by how disconnected from any sort of reality both the commentary and the suggestions for reform are.

It is relatively easy to dispose of the suggestions for reform. There is virtually no evidence they will work. That doesn't mean they are bad ideas per se, but just that they won't accomplish what their proponents intend.

Take, for instance, the proposal for more disclosure. In 1993, shareholder activist Ralph Whitworth closed down the advocacy group United Shareholders of America because, with SEC-mandated disclosure of many elements of compensation, he thought the problems with executive pay were over.[3] Companies complied with the mandates. Proxy statements expanded to include not just base pay but bonuses as well, and then expanded further to provide information on stock option grants, including the average stock price of the grant and what percentage of all options granted were given to the CEO. Did that disclosure curtail the size of grants? Not that I can see. Did disclosing the disproportional percentage of stock options obtained by the CEO cause a more equal distribution of option grants? I don't think so. If anything, all this public attention to the various components of pay may have set off an arms race, as executives were interested in not being worse off than their peers and the compensation of peers was ever more visible in the published disclosures. Not wanting to be worse off is the inevitable result of the social comparison process through which people assess how well they are being treated.

The change in the composition of compensation committees and the separation of the role of board chairperson from CEO, implemented several years ago, also did nothing that I can see to halt the rise in executive pay or to tie pay more tightly to performance. Comprehensive summaries of extensive empirical research find no evidence that board structure matters.[4] The basic idea underlying the reforms was to get more "independence" into the decision-making process. But psychological independence is a very different thing from legal independence or independence as a matter of organizational affiliation. Many board members have been brought onto the board by the CEO, and even if there is an independent corporate governance committee, it is highly unlikely that a board member will be added without the CEO's acquiescence. If board members work together, including with the CEO, it is unlikely that they are going to be dispassionate participants in the pay-setting process. Instead, their perceptions of what the CEO should be paid will invariably be affected by their relationship, either positive or negative, with that person.

Social influence and norms of reciprocity matter, as research on compensation by Charles O'Reilly has demonstrated.[5] If the various reforms have not worked in the past, there is no reason to believe they are going to work in the future.

Executive pay is invariably set through a process of benchmarking—comparing (loosely controlling for things like company size and industry) a focal company's pay with the pay of other companies. And setting pay through a process of benchmarking actually makes a lot of sense. Yale economist Bengt Holmstrom, who serves on the board of a closely held family company, has noted that because compensation is a sensitive matter, the board (and the CEO) want to avoid contentious, arm's-length bargaining that might poison the working relationship.[6] Using outside consultants and salary surveys helps in this regard.

But as Graef Crystal pointed out more than 15 years ago, this is a process that is going to inevitably produce a rise in average salaries over time.[7] That's because of the "above-average effect"— the tendency for all people to believe they are better than average with respect to judgments about all sorts of things ranging from income to negotiating ability to intelligence. Since CEOs are going to think they are above average, they are going to want to be paid at least the average for comparable CEOs. And, by the way, compensation committees and other board members aren't going to want to believe that *their* CEO is below average, because if that were the case, then they wouldn't be doing their job of hiring and firing executives effectively so the *board* would then be below average. Since, by definition, half of the people are paid below the median, the desire for *everyone* to be paid at least the average leads to a continual upward pressure on wage rates.

So why has CEO pay increased so rapidly and increasingly diverged from the pay of lower-level executives and rank-and-file employees? I believe there are a set of interrelated reasons. The first is a complex dynamic: CEOs are getting fired at a higher rate, which means that the average tenure of a CEO is declining and the reputational risk of being a CEO—being fired is not good for one's image—has increased. Booz Allen Hamilton reported that between 1995 and 2004, CEO turnover increased some 300 percent, and that dismissals of CEOs increased not just in North America but in Europe and Asia as well.[8] In 2005, some 15 percent of CEOs left office, and were as likely to leave prematurely as to retire normally.[9] If CEOs believe they are increasingly at risk for dismissal and that their tenures are going to be shorter, they are going to demand higher pay as a compensation in return. However, once companies pay their CEOs more money, they are going to have higher expectations for performance and less patience with underperformance, other things being equal. So, higher pay will drive more rapid dismissal, and more rapid dismissal will, in turn, drive demands for higher pay.

Second, it is far from clear that pay in public companies is actually too high, given the prevailing beliefs about the importance of CEOs to company success. One recent survey found that more than half of all board members expect both cash and stock compensation to continue to rise, and the Business Roundtable argues that compensation has simply kept pace with increases in company value.[10] That does not mean that CEOs are as crucial as conventional wisdom makes out, and in fact there are lots of reasons to think that leaders' impact is overestimated compared with forces affecting organizational performance such as the general economy and particular industry conditions.[11] But it does mean that if an organization and its board believe that the CEO is *the* factor that will make or break a company, they'll be willing to pay quite a bit to get the "right" person in the job. Harvard Business School professor Rakesh Khurana has referred to this behavior as "searching for a corporate savior," arguing that the belief in the potency of the CEO has led to a free-agent market for executive talent and an associated rise in CEO salaries.[12]

The belief in the potency and importance of the CEO has been driven, in part, by the business press, which has made CEOs into almost rock-star figures. Years ago, I doubt if many people could have named the CEOs of even large and prominent companies, but today, people like Apple's Steve Jobs, for instance, have almost iconic status. More business biographies and autobiographies are being written, because more people are increasingly interested in knowing about CEOs' lives and philosophies. And this celebrity status will then be reflected in the salaries paid to those individuals.

Yet other data suggest that CEO compensation is not necessarily unrealistic. One perceived problem—the disconnect between pay and performance—is easily explained. Pay is supposed to motivate behavior. Company performance goals are typically set on an annual basis, and compensation committees set their numbers based on these goals. But if it becomes clear about halfway through the year that, for whatever reason, the targets are not going to be met, arguments are made that if the executive team is to be motivated to do the best they can under the circumstances, the targets need to be changed. Readjusting the targets may motivate the team but invariably leads to this disconnect between pay and company performance.

And we would do well to look at the dramatic increase in the number of companies going private in leveraged buyout transactions. One reason for this trend, given by both organizational leaders and people in the private equity industry, is that the senior executive team can earn a bigger payday in private rather than public companies. If firms controlled by private equity companies, which have to be seen as the most activist of owners, actually pay CEOs of successful enterprises more than they would earn if the company were public, that suggests that CEO pay may not actually be too high. This is Bengt Holmstrom's implicit conclusion as well, when he noted that there was not much difference in the pay-setting process in a closely held, private company—where there is no issue of dispersed shareholders with inadequate power over the board and the pay determination process—than that observed in the typical public company.[13] So, my conclusion is that the supposed "problems" with executive pay may not actually be problems at all.

But if executive pay *is* going to be fundamentally changed, then two things will need to be altered. First, probably less disclosure, not more, is desirable. One might reasonably ask why the pay of lower level people has not also ratcheted up through the same social comparison process that occurs for CEO pay? I think one answer is that pay comparisons are more difficult to make for people farther down in the hierarchy. That's because pay secrecy is a common policy in many companies, and some even threaten employees with being fired if they discuss their pay with colleagues. With secret pay and prohibitions on discussions of comparative pay, the social comparison dynamic is short-circuited.

Second, as long as people believe that corporate performance is the result of what the CEO does, the CEO-as-celebrity culture will persist and boards will tend to overpay the CEO. So, ending the CEO pay conundrum will require overcoming the "fundamental attribution error," the tendency to overattribute causality to the characteristics and actions of individuals as compared to the situations in which they are acting. Since this is such a fundamental psychological principle, I wouldn't hold my breath.

CHAPTER 28

Stopping Corporate Misdeeds

How We Teach the Wrong Lessons

AT A DINNER A FEW YEARS AGO with Silicon Valley executives, I heard some amazing things. After first bemoaning the wave of corporate scandals, one person after another explained how their companies had found ways to "extend" their quarters to make their numbers. In other words, if the quarter ended on June 30 and they needed more sales to meet analyst targets, the quarter might be extended and the books held open another day or two. What's interesting is that none of the executives saw anything particularly wrong with this.

Meanwhile, a Korean friend who used to work as a senior manager at SK Global, wondered what would happen when its parent company, South Korean SK Corporation, fell into financial difficulty through a series of illegal stock trades and a number of its senior executives, including the chairman, went to jail. Would he become "damaged goods," tarnished by his company's misdeeds? He was surprised to find that people actually seemed *more* eager than ever to meet with him. Apparently, since there had been billions of dollars at stake in SK's financial machinations, people thought he might have access to some of the loot. Sort of makes you wonder.

Is the ethical behavior of business leaders worse today than it was in the past? That's a hard one to answer. The last decade has seen dozens of corporate scandals, ranging from the accounting frauds at WorldCom, Enron, Cendant, HealthSouth, and Informix, to the backdating of stock option grants at Brocade Communications, Comverse Technology, and Apple Computer to the trading on inside information at ImClone, where Martha Stewart got swept up in the investigation. Clearly, business behavior is not what it should be. Some of the bad behavior occurred in companies led by MBAs, such as Jeff Skilling and Andrew Fastow at Enron. In response, business schools have added courses on ethics and companies have instituted more ethics training, with some even appointing a chief ethics officer. There are differences of opinion as to whether ethical standards can be taught in a classroom, whether they are formed relatively early in life under parental influence, and if teachable, what is the best way to teach them.

But if ethics are developed and learned in school, or for that matter, if ethical standards result from what happens to those who bend the rules in business, we are definitely in trouble. Consider first the evidence from schools. Research conducted by Don McCabe and Linda Trevino, among others, as well as extensive anecdotal evidence indicates that cheating among college students has increased over the years to truly shocking levels. A 2005 report on a survey of 50,000 undergraduates on some 60 campuses found that 70 percent admitted to some cheating, and there is evidence that both plagiarism and giving unpermitted aid on examinations or assignments are increasing in frequency.[1] And research shows that cheating among business school students exceeds the rate of cheating of any other college major.[2] What's going on?

I think an important cause of the sorry state of ethical behavior is the consequences—or more precisely, the absence thereof—of such behavior. As learning theorist B. F. Skinner once argued, behavior is a function of its consequences.[3] So, let's examine the consequences of various forms of malfeasance in both companies and colleges.

Consider first the case of college cheating. Stanford has an honor code that students sign on every exam, in which they affirm that they will neither give nor receive aid and that they have an obligation to uphold the honor code by bringing violations to the attention of people in authority. But the enforcement and reality of the honor code is quite different from the official proclamations. I attended a Stanford Business School faculty meeting in which a colleague told the assembled group in no uncertain terms that if they observed or suspected cheating in their class, there was only one rational response: do nothing! Having pursued a suspected honor code violation, my colleague had put in endless hours of effort and been subject to the antipathy of the accused and their student colleagues—to very little result.

When I talked to Stanford's judicial affairs officer about cheating, here is what she told me. First of all, Stanford seems to be a micro version of McCabe and Trevino's broader national sample—the level of cheating has increased. This is due in part to the pressure from parents, peers, graduate schools, and the students themselves to succeed in a highly competitive environment. In addition, students have learned, in their cultures and in their previous education, that the ends justify the means. A third factor has to do with the reasons students pursue higher education. The importance of learning is sometimes subordinated to earning a credential that can get one a good job or put one on a path to career success. McCabe and Trevino's research has found that, not surprisingly, students who are interested in education primarily for instrumental reasons are more likely to cheat than those who are intrinsically interested in the subject matter. That explains their finding for business school students: as the most instrumentally oriented toward their education, they are more likely to bend the rules of academic integrity.

Yet another contributing cause is the Internet, which has made cheating easier—you can buy term papers online, for instance. In an ironic turn, Internet-based cheating has stimulated the creation of such businesses such Turnitin.com that, for a fee, help instructors identify cheating facilitated by the Web. One can just picture the sort of dueling software—sort of like video and music piracy—where sites that help people cheat try to outsmart Turnitin, while the service must continually sharpen its detection tools and methods.

But the big problem is that not much happens if students cheat. Students, honor code notwithstanding, are unlikely to "snitch" and turn in their peers. Most students I know are very concerned with peer acceptance, with building a social network with their fellow students that they will rely on in the future, and with acting according to the prevailing cultural norms. Faculty members have every incentive to look the other way rather than expend time and energy on suspected instances of cheating. What's in it for them to do otherwise? That's why surveys of some 10,000 faculty members by the Center for Academic Integrity found that 44 percent of those who were aware of student cheating in their courses have *never* reported a student for cheating.[4]

And if cheating is proved beyond a shadow of a doubt, the penalty is often quite mild, typically a one-quarter suspension and 40 hours of community service, at least at Stanford. When I asked what it took to actually get thrown out of Stanford, the answer I got was, "Quite a lot." Five people had been thrown out in the preceding five years. One had plagiarized the doctoral dissertation and forged the adviser's signature (either one by itself would probably not have been sufficient for expulsion). One had been thrown out for sexual assault, but by the time he was separated from Stanford, he was already incarcerated in a California jail. Another had engaged repeatedly in proscribed behavior. And so it went.

When I inquired as to why the penalties were so seemingly mild, the response was that Stanford was an educational institution and that as such emphasized remediation and rehabilitation rather than punishment. Of course, between mild sanctions and the small proportion of cheating that actually gets investigated, Stanford, like virtually all of its peer institutions, actually *is* teaching students something—that cheating is not that big a deal.

And lest you be horrified by the lax enforcement of ethical standards on college campuses, consider what happens to corporate miscreants. I'm not talking about the occasional fine or jail term. I'm talking about whether or not serious corporate misbehavior seems to matter at all to the people who are the most important—the accused individual's peers.

There I am with my wife at a post-Christmas party at the home of a friend who personally is quite religious and very ethical. At the party is Phil White, apparently a friend of the host. White was the former CEO of Informix, a software company that got into deep trouble for inflating its revenues. White lost his job and was indicted, convicted, and ultimately sentenced to jail; the company was sued, its stock price plummeted, and eventually it changed its name and was sold. The point? I doubt very much if our host would have invited a convicted thief, murderer, or sex offender, regardless of the preexisting personal relationship. But white-collar crime? No big deal.

At another dinner party we were regaled with the host's close relationship with Martha Stewart—after Stewart had been convicted and served some jail time. Keith Ferrazzi, a marketing guru, worked as CEO of YaYa, an Internet-gaming marketing company funded in part by Michael Milken. Milken, who virtually invented junk bonds at Drexel Burnham, served time in jail, and paid a $500 million fine for securities law violations. The fine and jail have clearly not terminally hurt Milken's rehabilitation and return to the business world; in fact, Milken implied in a comment to Ferrazzi that the notoriety actually helped open doors, because people had heard of him. I certainly believe in rehabilitation, and there is no point in keeping talented individuals from exercising their gifts and skills in their chosen profession forever because of an ethical or legal lapse—*once they have paid the penalty*. And in this respect, one cannot help be struck by the contrast between what happens to those accused and convicted of "white collar" crimes and those accused and convicted of "conventionally" criminal misdeeds.

Social reactions and acceptance matter a lot. People are social animals. That's why the most severe punishment meted out at the military academies, short of dismissal, is ostracism. That's why solitary confinement in prison is considered a "step up" in the level of punishment. As social beings, we care deeply about what others think of us. Obviously, people with large egos—and that includes many entrepreneurs and CEOs—are concerned about their reputations, how they appear to others, whether or not they are well regarded. So, social approval or disapproval is an important reward or punishment. The incidents I've recounted illustrate a remarkably consistent picture. Just as there is little likelihood of getting caught and relatively mild sanctions for cheating in college, there are relatively mild *social* sanctions for engaging in various forms of business crime. There may be many reasons for this. One of the most obvious is the attraction of power and money. People are so strongly drawn to these things and those who possess them that they may not think too much about the ethical issues. But I think one big cause of our lenience is that the competitive climate of both business schools and the corporate world valorizes the adage "the ends justify the means"—that the results, not how they are achieved, are all that matters. So people are willing to overlook questionable actions—if they even recognize anything to overlook.

But something is lost in all of this acceptance of bad behavior. Turning in someone else's work or copying on an exam may help get a higher grade, but it represents a fundamental separation of the individual from his or her work. Fudging sales numbers or keeping the books open longer at the end of the quarter may temporarily help a company make its numbers, but such actions are inconsistent with a company actually standing by and taking pride in its real performance and accomplishments. There was a time when companies and people took pride in what they did and how they did it—not just in the results toted up on some financial Ouija board but in the processes that produced those results. Returning to the idea that *what* people and companies *do*, not just what they *achieve*, matters is the first and most important step on the road to more ethical clarity and higher standards of behavior. But what do I know? I still do my own writing.

Notes

Chapter 2

1. http://pewtrusts.com/idea/idea_item.cfm?conetent_item_id= 1010.

2. "Bad Customer Service Is Top Reason Consumers Switch Carriers," http://www.mobilemedia.com/news/33661.html.

3. "UK Customers Fed Up with Bad Customer Service," April 25, 2006, http://www.businesszone.co.uk/cgi-bin/item.cgi?id=154021&d=1009 &h=10008&f=10.

4. "Survey: Young Adults Tolerate, Expect Bad Customer Service," February 8, 2006, http://multichannelmerchant.com/opsandfulfillment /advisor/teens_tolerate/

5. See, for example, Frederick F. Reichheld, *The Loyalty Effect* (Boston: Harvard Business School Press, 1996); Frederick F. Reichheld, *Loyalty Rules! How Today's Leaders Build Lasting Relationships* (Boston: Harvard Business School Press, 2001).

6. "Gartner Says CRM Spending to Reach $76.3 Billion in 2005," Gartner press release, 2001.

7. "CRM Spending and Trends," eMarketer, Inc., 2005.

8. "Most Retailers Will Boost CRM Spending Over Next 2 Years, NRF Study Says," *Internet Retailer*, March 20, 2003.

9. "Spending on Customer Service Technology Will Outpace Other IT Initiatives," Jupiter Media Metrix, press release, February 25, 2002.

10. Jan Carlzon, *Moments of Truth* (Boston: Ballinger, 1987).

11. "Supermarket Hiring: Labor Quality's Impact on the Bottom Line," www.unicru.com.

12. Bill Clarke's "Common Sense Series #5, The Customer Perspective: The Final 3 Feet" can be found at http://where-its-at.com in the October 30, 2001, issue of the newsletter.

Chapter 3

1. Transcript of author interview with Ed Ossie, June 2006.
2. See, for instance, E. E. Kossek and C. Ozeki, "Work-Family Conflict, Policies, and the Job-Life Satisfaction Relationship: A Review and Directions for Organizational Behavior-Human Resources Research," *Journal of Applied Psychology* 83 (1998): 139–149.
3. Scott L. Boyar, Carl P. Maertz, Jr., and Allison W. Pearson, "The Effects of Work-Family Conflict and Family-Work Conflict on Nonattendance Behaviors," *Journal of Business Research* 58 (July 2005): 919–925.

Chapter 4

1. Floyd Norris, "U.S. Tech Exports Slide, But Trash Sales Are Up," *New York Times*, January 14, 2005, C1.
2. "Mirror, Mirror on the Wall," *The Economist*, June 17, 2004.
3. U.S. Census Bureau, *Statistical Abstract of the United States: 2001*, 319.
4. "A Citizen's Guide to the Federal Budget, Fiscal Year 1996," http://www.gpoaccess.gov/usbudget/citizensguide.html, 6.
5. Edmund L. Andrews, "Why U.S. Companies Shouldn't Whine About Taxes," *New York Times*, July 9, 2006, BU3.
6. Marcus Walker, "Most Competitive? Nordic Nations Trump China," *Wall Street Journal*, October 14, 2004, A17.
7. Richard Florida, "America's Looming Creativity Crisis," *Harvard Business Review*, October 2004, 124.
8. Ibid.
9. Ibid., 126.
10. Economist Intelligence Unit, "Scattering the Seeds of Invention: The Globalisation of Research and Development," Economist Intelligence Unit, September 2004, 2.
11. Diana Jean Schemo, "A Third of U.S. Dropouts Never Reach 10th Grade," *New York Times,* June 21, 2006, A16.

12. "Most Young People Entering the U.S. Workforce Lack Critical Skills Essential for Success." The Conference Board press release, October 2, 2006.

13. "It's 2008: Do You Know Where Your Talent Is?" Deloitte research paper (New York: Deloitte Development LLC, 2004), 3.

14. Henry Blodget, "Consider the Outsource," *New York Times Book Review*, July 3, 2005, 14.

15. M. Lemke, S. Sen, E. Pahlke, L. Partelow, D. Miller, T. Williams, D. Kastberg, and L. Jocelyn, *International Outcomes of Learning Mathematics Literacy and Problem Solving: PISA 2003 Results from the U.S. Perspective* (Washington, DC: U.S. Department of Education, National Center for Education Statistics, 2004).

16. National Center for Education Statistics, *Highlights from the 2000 Program for International Student Assessment (PISA)* (Washington, DC: U.S. Department of Education, Office of Educational Research and Improvement, 2002).

17. Blodget, "Consider the Outsource."

18. Robert Levering and Milton Moskowitz, "The 100 Best Companies to Work For," *Fortune*, January 12, 2004.

19. Winfred Arthur Jr., Winston Bennett Jr., Pamela S. Edens, and Suzanne T. Bel, "Effectiveness of Training in Organizations: A Meta-Analysis of Design and Evaluation Features," *Journal of Applied Psychology* 88 (2003): 234–245.

20. John M. Barron, Dan A. Black, and Mark A. Lowenstein, "Job Matching and On-the-Job Training," *Journal of Labor Economics* 7 (1989): 1–19.

21. Wayne F. Cascio, "The Economic Impact of Employee Behaviors on Organizational Performance," *California Management Review* 48 (Summer 2006): 41–59.

Chapter 5

1. The discussion of organizational learning in hospitals can be found in Amy C. Edmondson, "Learning from Mistakes Is Easier Said Than Done: Group and Organizational Influences on the Detection and Correction of Human Errors," *Journal of Applied Behavioral Science* 32 (1996): 5–28; and Anita L. Tucker and Amy C. Edmondson, "Why

Hospitals Don't Learn from Failures: Organizational and Psychological Dynamics That Inhibit System Change," *California Management Review* 45 (2003): 55–72.

2. Jody Hoffer Gittell, *The Southwest Airlines Way* (New York: McGraw-Hill, 2003).

3. Jeffrey Pfeffer, "Human Resources at the AES Corporation: The Case of the Missing Department," Case no. HR-3 (Stanford, CA: Graduate School of Business, Stanford University, November 2004).

4. A nice description of innovation and the role of technology brokering can be found in Andrew Hargadon, *How Breakthroughs Happen: The Surprising Truth About How Companies Innovate* (Boston: Harvard Business School Press, 2003).

5. Atul Gawande, *Complications* (New York: Henry Holt, 2002).

Chapter 6

1. For example, see Harvey Seifter, "The Conductor-less Orchestra," *Leader to Leader* 21 (Summer 2001), http://www.leadertoleader.org /knowledgecenter/L2L/index.html#summer01.

2. "Headless," Economist.com, August 3, 2006.

3. Ibid.

4. Seifter, "The Conductor-less Orchestra."

5. Richard Dyer, "Orpheus Artists Are in Tune with One Another," *Boston Globe*, February 1, 2005.

6. Vivien Schweitzer, "Orpheus Goes to School," *Symphony* 57 (September–October 2006): 40.

7. James Surowiecki, *The Wisdom of Crowds* (New York: Random House, 2004).

8. See, for instance, Rosemary Batt, "The Economics of Teams Among Technicians," *British Journal of Industrial Relations* 39 (2001): 1–25; Rosemary Batt, "The Outcomes of Self-Directed Teams in Services," paper presented in the session on "Work Redesign in the Service Sector," *Proceedings of the Forty-Eighth Annual Meeting of the IRRA* (Madison, WI: IRRA Series, 1996).

9. Rakesh Khurana, *Searching for a Corporate Savior: The Irrational Quest for Charismatic CEOs* (Princeton, NJ: Princeton University Press, 2002).

10. Morgan W. McCall, *High Flyers: Developing the Next Generation of Leaders* (Boston: Harvard Business School Press, 1998.)

Chapter 7

1. Barbara De Lollis, "Airline Workers Branch Out to Make Ends Meet," *USA Today*, October 21, 2004.

2. Fay Hansen, "Low Wage Nation," *Workforce Management*, June 2005, 87.

3. "Survey Finds Flying Cheap Can Be Best," CNN.com, April 5, 2004.

4. Joe Sharkey, "Cheap Fares to Europe? Don't Get Him Started," *New York Times*, July 5, 2005, C6.

5. Paul A. Eisenstein, "Toyota, GM Tops in '05 Harbour Report," http://www.thecarconnection.com/Industry_News_Toyota, July 1, 2005.

6. Ibid. According to the 2005 Harbour Report, it took Toyota 27.90 labor hours per vehicle while it took Ford Motor 36.98 hours. That 9.08-hour difference means Ford's time to assemble is 32.5 percent higher than Toyota's.

7. Scott McCartney, "How Discount Airlines Profited from Their Bigger Rival's Woes," *Wall Street Journal*, August 12, 2004, A1.

8. Airlinepilotpay.com (accessed spring 2004; this Web site is now inactive).

9. Micheline Maynard, "An Early Push on Fall Sales by Airlines," *New York Times*, July 13, 2004, C1.

10. Patrick J. Kiger, "Thinking Like an Investor," *Workforce Management*, June 2006, 37–39.

Chapter 8

1. "Data Bank," *Workforce Management*, February 2006, 22.

2. Phyllis Feinberg, "Defined Benefit Pension Plans Falling Out of Favor," *Business Insurance*, May 17, 2004, 46.

3. http://www.definityhealth.com/marketing/index.html.

4. K. Anders Ericsson, *The Road to Excellence: The Acquisition of Expert Performance in the Arts and Sciences, Sports, and Games* (New York: Earlbaum, 1996).

5. Sheena S. Iyengar, Wei Jiang, and Gur Huberman, "How Much Choice Is Too Much? Determinants of Individual Contributions in 401K Retirement Plans," in *Pension Design and Structure: New Lessons from Behavioral Finance*, eds. Olivia S. Mitchell and Stephen P. Utkus (Oxford: Oxford University Press, 2004), 83–95.

6. Ieva M. Augstums, "Gen X, Y Workers Weight HMOs, PPOs and HSAs," *Dallas Morning News*, October 24, 2005.

7. Nicole L. Torres, "Healthy Returns," *Entrepreneur*, April 2005, 118.

8. Theo Francis, "Escape from Claims Hell," *Wall Street Journal*, March 20, 2006, R8.

9. Sanford Jacoby, *Modern Manors: Welfare Capitalism Since the New Deal* (Princeton, NJ: Princeton University Press, 1997).

Chapter 9

1. Websense, "Flexibility: The Evolution of Employee Internet Management," November 2000.

2. AMA/ePolicy Institute Research, summary in "2005 Electronic Monitoring & Surveillance Survey."

3. Jane Simms, "And Another Thing . . . ," *Director*, August 2005, 27.

4. Wayne F. Cascio, "The Economic Impact of Employee Behaviors on Organizational Performance," *California Management Review* 48 (Summer 2006): 41–59.

5. John R. Aiello and Yang Shao, "Electronic Performance Monitoring and Stress: The Role of Feedback and Goal Setting," in *Human Computer Interaction: Applications and Case Studies*, eds. Michael J. Smith and Gavriel Salvendy (Amsterdam: Elsevier Science, 1993), 1011–1016.

6. Elizabeth A. Douthitt and John R. Aiello, "The Role of Participation and Control in the Effects of Computer Monitoring on Fairness Perceptions, Task Satisfaction, and Performance," *Journal of Applied Psychology* 86 (2001): 867–874.

7. Jack W. Brehm, *A Theory of Psychological Reactance* (New York: Academic Press, 1966).

8. Both the principles of reactance and scarcity are described in Robert B. Cialdini, *Influence: Science and Practice* (Glenview, IL: Scott, Foresman, 1988).

9. John H. Lingle, Timothy C. Brock, and Robert B. Cialdini, "Surveillance Instigates Entrapment When Violations Are Observed: When Personal Involvement Is High, and When Sanctions Are Severe." *Journal of Personality and Social Psychology* 35 (1977): 419–429.

10. L. H. Strickland, "Surveillance and Trust," *Journal of Personality* 26 (1958): 200–215; A. W. Kruglanski, "Attributing Trustworthiness in Supervisor-Worker Relations," *Journal of Experimental Social Psychology* 6 (1970): 214–232.

Chapter 10

1. Timothy Egan, "The Rise of Shrinking-Vacation Syndrome," *New York Times*, August 20, 2006, 18.

2. "Mirror, Mirror on the Wall," *The Economist*, June 17, 2004.

3. Ibid.

4. Anne Spurgeon, *Working Time: Its Impact on Safety and Health* (Geneva: International Labour Office, 2003), 24.

5. Del Jones, "America Loves to Hate Dastardly CEOs," http://www.usatoday.com/educate/college/careers/news14.htm.

6. Spurgeon, *Working Time*, chapter 4.

7. *The World Health Report 2000—Health Systems: Improving Performance* (Geneva: World Health Organization, 2000). The WHO Web site has numerous statistics on comparative health care expenditures and outcomes.

8. "It's 2008: Do You Know Where Your Talent Is?" Deloitte research paper (New York: Deloitte Development LLC, 2004).

9. Egan, "The Rise of Shrinking-Vacation Syndrome."

10. Richard Florida, *The Flight of the Creative Class: The New Global Competition for Talent* (New York: Harper Collins, 2005).

Chapter 11

1. "Garbage Truck Drivers Rushing to Finish Routes Are a Safety Risk," Associated Press, January 30, 2004.

2. Ellen G. Rank, "Trends in Incentive Compensation," information furnished to the author by Hewitt Associates in June 2004.

3. "Christmas Bonuses Give Way to Incentive Pay," *Edmonton Journal*, November 28, 2003.

4. See, for instance, Diana Jean Schemo, "When Students' Gains Help Teachers' Bottom Line," *New York Times*, May 9, 2004.

5. "Results-Oriented Cultures: Creating a Clear Linkage Between Individual Performance and Organizational Success," GAO-03-488 (Washington, DC: General Accounting Office, March 2003).

6. Bryan Jacob and Steven D. Levitt, "Rotten Apples: An Investigation of Prevalence and Predictors of Teacher Cheating," working paper 9413, National Bureau of Economic Research, New York, 2002.

7. Floyd Norris, "Stock Options: Do They Make Bosses Cheat?" *New York Times*, August 8, 2005.

8. There is a great discussion of and evidence on the extrinsic incentives bias in Chip Heath, "On the Social Psychology of Agency Relationships: Lay Theories of Motivation Overemphasize Extrinsic Incentives," *Organizational Behavior and Human Decision Processes* 78 (1999): 25–62.

9. George Zimmer, guest lecture (Stanford, CA: Graduate School of Business, Stanford University, May 14, 1998), VHS.

Chapter 12

1. Milt Freudenheim, "A New Worry for Investors: Retirees' Medical Benefits," *New York Times*, July 25, 2005.

2. Ellen E. Schultz, "Widow's Lament," *Wall Street Journal*, June 29, 2005, B1, B3.

3. Vineeta Anand, "Group Claims Defined Benefit Plans Being Strangled by Poor Rules, Laws," *Pensions & Investments*, June 14, 2004, 18.

4. Sally Roberts, "More Employers Freezing, Phasing Out DB Pensions," *Business Insurance*, August 30, 2004, 114.

5. Ibid.

6. "Boomer Backlash: Controversy Besetting New Pension Plan Rises with IBM's Retreat—Cash Balance System's Effect on Older Workers Stirs IRS, Congress, EEOC," *Wall Street Journal*, September 20, 1999, A1.

7. Jessica Marquez, "IBM Strives for the Security of Defined-Benefit Programs as It Shifts Focus to 401(k)s," *Workforce Management*, June 2005, 79.

8. Charles Forelle, "Stingier Health Plans Create Risks: Many Patients Stop Taking Medications When Faced with Higher Co-Payments," *Wall Street Journal*, December 4, 2003, D3.

9. www.discoverysurveys.com.

10. Towers Perrin HR Services, "Working Today: Understanding What Drives Employee Engagement," 2003.

11. Fay Hansen, "Managing the New World Order," *Workforce Management*, July 2006, 18.

Chapter 13

1. Andrea Kay, "Job Hunting: Lying on Resumes," http://www.andreakay.com/jobhunting/art_1067.htm.

2. Al Lewis, "Some Work at Lying to Get a Good Job," DenverPost.com, March 28, 2006.

3. Kris Frieswick, "Liar, Liar—Grapevine—Lying on Resumes," *CFO: Magazine for Senior Financial Executives*, December 2002.

4. Kay, "Job Hunting."

5. Ibid.

6. Dr. Laurence J. Peter and Raymond Hull, *The Peter Principle: Why Things Always Go Wrong* (New York: William Morrow, 1969).

7. Roger Martin, *The Responsibility Virus* (New York: Basic Books, 2002).

8. Jennifer A. Chatman, "Managing People and Organizations: Selection and Socialization in Public Accounting Firms," *Administrative Science Quarterly* 36 (1991): 459–484.

Chapter 14

1. Jim Collins, *Good to Great* (New York: HarperBusiness, 2001).

2. Victoria Chang and Jeffrey Pfeffer, "Keith Ferrazzi," Case no. OB-44 (Stanford, CA: Graduate School of Business, Stanford University, October 2003).

3. Keith Ferrazzi and Tahl Raz, *Never Eat Alone* (New York: Doubleday Currency, 2005).

4. There are literally scores of discussions and studies of the principle of commitment. See, for example, Robert B. Cialdini, *Influence:*

Science and Practice (Glenview, IL: Scott, Foresman, 1988); Gerald R. Salancik, "Commitment and the Control of Organizational Behavior and Belief," in *New Directions in Organizational Behavior*, eds. Barry M. Staw and Gerald R. Salancik (Chicago: St. Clair Press, 1977), 1–21.

5. Robert B. Cialdini, Richard J. Borden, Avril Thorne, Marcus R. Walker, Steven Freeman, and Lloyd R. Sloan, "Basking in Reflected Glory: Three (Football) Field Studies," *Journal of Personality and Social Psychology* 34 (1976): 366–375.

6. David Rensin, *The Mailroom: Hollywood History from the Bottom Up* (New York: Ballantine, 2003).

7. Joel M. Podolny, "A Status-Based Model of Market Competition," *American Journal of Sociology* 98 (January 1993): 829–872.

8. Walter Isaacson, *Kissinger: A Biography* (New York: Simon and Schuster, 1992).

9. Robert A. Caro, *The Path to Power* (New York: Knopf, 1981).

10. Eddie Pells, "Spurrier Resigns as Football Coach," Associated Press, January 4, 2001.

Chapter 15

1. Tessa R. Salazar, "World's Biggest Automaker Revs Up Asia Pacific," *Philippine Daily Inquirer*, January 19, 2005.

2. See, for instance, Elizabeth Kolbert, "How Tina Brown Moves Magazines," *New York Times Magazine*, December 5, 1993.

3. Jeffrey Pfeffer, *Managing with Power* (Boston: Harvard Business School Press, 1992); see particularly pages 286–287.

4. From the transcript of a talk given by Andy Grove at a Harvard Business School Publishing conference in Cupertino, California, October 3, 2002.

Chapter 16

1. Robert B. Cialdini, *Influence: The Psychology of Persuasion*, rev. ed. (New York: HarperCollins, 1998).

2. John Heilemann, "Who Speaks for Tech?" *Business 2.0*, September 2003.

3. Connie Bruck, "The Personal Touch," *The New Yorker*, August 13, 2001, 42–59.

4. Jeffrey Pfeffer, "How to Turn On the Charm," *Business 2.0*, June 2004, 76.

5. George Anders, "The Best Acquisitions Start with a CEO Who Charms Sellers," *Wall Street Journal*, August 21, 2006, B1.

6. See, for instance, Jerry M. Burger, Shelley Soroka, Katrina Gonzago, Emily Murphy, and Emily Somervell, "The Effect of Fleeting Attraction on Compliance to Requests," *Personality and Social Psychology Bulletin* 27 (2001): 1578–1586.

7. Bruck, "The Personal Touch."

8. Correspondence with author.

Chapter 17

1. John Paul MacDuffie, "The Road to 'Root Cause': Shop-Floor Problem-Solving at Three Auto Assembly Plants," *Management Science* 43 (April 1997), 479–502. The discussion of the "actual part, actual situation" process appears on page 492. See also John Paul MacDuffie and Susan Helper, "Creating Lean Suppliers: Diffusing Lean Production Through the Supply Chain," *California Management Review* 39 (Summer 1997): 118–151.

Chapter 18

1. Howard S. Schwartz, *Narcissistic Process and Corporate Decay: The Theory of the Organization Ideal* (New York: New York University Press, 1992).

2. Fiona Lee, Christopher Peterson, and Larissa Z. Tiedens, "Mea Culpa: Predicting Stock Prices from Organizational Attributions," *Personality and Social Psychology Bulletin* 30 (December 2004): 1636–1649.

3. See, for instance, J. R. Bettman and B. A. Weitz, "Attributions in the Board Room: Causal Reasoning in Corporate Annual Reports," *Administrative Science Quarterly* 28 (1983): 165–183; G. R. Salancik and J. R. Meindl, "Corporate Attributions as Strategic Illusions of Management Control," *Administrative Science Quarterly* 29 (1984): 238–254.

4. Lee, Peterson, and Tiedens, "Mea Culpa."

5. Christo Boshoff and Jason Leong, "Empowerment, Attribution and Apologising as Dimensions of Service Recovery: An Experimental Study," *International Journal of Service Industry Management* 9 (1998): 24–47.

6. Cinda Becker, "Accepting Responsibility," *Modern Healthcare,* August 6, 2001, 4–5.

Chapter 19

1. Most books on talent and talent management, and there are many, emphasize "smarts." See, as one exemplar, Ed Michaels, Helen Handfield-Jones, and Beth Axelrod, *The War for Talent* (Boston: Harvard Business School Press, 2001).

2. Brooke A. Masters, *Spoiling for a Fight: The Rise of Eliot Spitzer* (New York: Times Books/Henry Holt, 2006).

3. James Richardson, *Willie Brown: A Biography* (Berkeley: University of California Press, 1996).

4. Bernie Marcus and Arthur Blank, *Built from Scratch* (New York: Times Business, 1999), xv.

5. Quoted in Jeffrey Sonnenfeld and Andrew Ward, *Firing Back* (Boston: Harvard Business School Press, 2007). This book tells a number of stories of personal resilience from both the political and corporate arenas.

6. Phone interview with Sanjay Chakrabarty, June 26, 2006.

7. Ted Baker and Reed E. Nelson, "Creating Something from Nothing: Resource Construction Through Entrepreneurial Bricolage," *Administrative Science Quarterly* 50 (September 2005): 329–366.

Chapter 20

1. Victoria Chang and Jeffrey Pfeffer, "Dr. Laura Esserman (A)," Case no. OB-42 (Stanford, CA: Graduate School of Business, Stanford University, September 2003).

Chapter 21

1. Jeremy Hope and Robin Fraser, *Beyond Budgeting: How Managers Can Break Free from the Annual Performance Trap* (Boston: Harvard Business School Press, 2003), 6.

2. Marshall Loeb, "Jack Welch Lets Fly on Budgets, Bonuses, and Buddy Boards," *Fortune*, May 29, 1995, 73.

Chapter 22

1. "The NIRI Compensation Survey: An Assessment of Responsibilities, Staffing, and Salaries of Investor Relations Practitioners," National Investor Relations Institute, June 2005, 15.

2. Ibid., 8, 20.

3. The CEO Project, "Interviews with CEOs of Fast-Growth Companies, Summary of Findings, Preliminary Results as of 10/16/04," 14.

4. Patricia Robinson and Norihiko Shimizu, "Japanese Corporate Restructuring: CEO Priorities as a Window on Environmental and Organizational Change," *Academy of Management Perspectives* 20 (2006): 44–75.

5. Bruce N. Pfau and Ira T. Kay, *The Human Capital Edge: 21 People Management Practices Your Company Must Implement (or Avoid) to Maximize Shareholder Value* (New York: McGraw-Hill, 2002).

6. "An Analysis of Trends in the Practice of Investor Relations: Fifth Measurement," National Investor Relations Institute, August 2004, 11.

7. Measurement of intelligence: see Arthur R. Jensen, *The g Factor: The Science of Mental Ability* (Westport, CT: Praeger, 1998); R. B. Cattell, "The Measurement of Adult Intelligence," *Psychological Bulletin* 40 (1943): 153–193; measurement of personality dimensions: see, for instance, Barry M. Staw and Yochi Cohen-Charash, "The Dispositional Approach to Job Satisfaction: More Than a Mirage, Less Than an Oasis," *Journal of Organizational Behavior* 26 (2005): 59–78.

8. Jeffrey Pfeffer, "Shareholder Return Is the Wrong Measure," *Business 2.0*, August 2003, 77.

9. Baruch Lev, "On the Usefulness of Earnings and Earnings Research: Lessons and Directions from Two Decades of Empirical Research," *Journal of Accounting Research* 27 (Supplement, 1989): 153–192; Baruch Lev and Paul Zarowin, "The Boundaries of Financial Reporting and How to Extend Them," *Journal of Accounting Research* 37 (1999): 353–385.

10. Lev and Zarowin, "The Boundaries of Financial Reporting," 355.

11. D. Burgstahler and I. Dichev, "Earnings Management to Avoid Earnings Decreases and Losses," *Journal of Accounting and Economics* 24 (1997): 99–126.

12. Ron Kasznik and Maureen F. McNichols, "Does Meeting Earnings Expectations Matter? Evidence from Analyst Forecast Revisions and Share Prices," *Journal of Accounting Research* 40 (June 2002): 727–759.

13. Emily Chasan, "Investors Warn Against War on Guidance," *Yahoo! News*, July 29, 2006.

Chapter 23

1. For a nice discussion of the absence of differentiation in business schools, see Joyce Doria, Horacio Rozanski, and Ed Cohen, "What Business Needs from Business Schools," *Strategy + Business*, Issue 32 (2003): 39–45.

2. Fare data were gathered from Expedia.com on November 13, 2006, assuming a departure date of Monday, December 11, 2006 and a return on Wednesday, December 20, 2006.

3. Jon Birger, "The 30 Best Stocks from 1972 to 2002," *Money*, Fall 2002, 88–95.

4. Michael E. Porter, *Competitive Strategy* (New York: Free Press, 1981).

Chapter 24

1. See, for instance, Gregor Andrade, Mark Mitchell, and Erik Stafford, "New Evidence and Perspectives on Mergers," *Journal of Economic Perspectives* 15 (2001): 103–120; Michael C. Jensen and Richard S. Ruback, "The Market for Corporate Control: The Scientific Evidence," *Journal of Financial Economics* 11 (1983): 5050; Sara B. Moeller, Frederik P. Schlingermann, and Rene M. Stulz, "Firm Size and the Gains from Acquisitions, *Journal of Financial Economics* 73 (August 2004): 201–228.

2. David R. King, Dan K. Dalton, Catherine M. Daily, and Jeffrey G. Covin, "Meta-Analysis of Post Acquisition Performance: Indicators of Unidentified Moderators," *Strategic Management Journal* 25 (February 2004): 187–200.

3. The literature on self-enhancement, its mechanisms and causes, and how to diminish the tendency to self-enhance is vast. See, for instance, Joachim Krueger, "Enhancement Bias in Descriptions of Self and Others," *Personality and Social Psychology Bulletin* 24 (1998): 505–516.

4. Matthew L. A. Hayward and Donald C. Hambrick, "Explaining the Premium Paid for Large Acquisitions: Evidence of CEO Hubris," *Administrative Science Quarterly* 42 (March 1997): 103–127.

5. See the discussion of this issue in Jeffrey Pfeffer, *The Human Equation: Building Profits by Putting People First* (Boston: Harvard Business School Press, 1998), chapter 1.

Chapter 25

1. Michael Schrage, "Need Innovation? Start by Locking Up the Tech Toys," *Fortune*, December 18, 2000.

2. Edward Tufte, "PowerPoint Is Evil," *Wired*, September 2003, www.wired.com/wired/archive/11.09/ppt2.html.

3. See, for instance, Jeffrey Pfeffer and Robert I. Sutton, *The Knowing-Doing Gap: How Smart Companies Turn Knowledge into Action* (Boston: Harvard Business School Press, 2000), chapter 2.

4. The National Association of Corporate Directors, *Report of the NACD Blue Ribbon Commission on the Role of the Board in Corporate Strategy* (Washington, DC: NACD, 2004).

5. A partial review of this evidence can be found in Jeffrey Pfeffer and Robert I. Sutton, *Hard Facts, Dangerous Half-Truths, and Total Nonsense: Profiting from Evidence-Based Management* (Boston: Harvard Business School Press, 2006), chapter 6.

6. G. Bruce Knecht, "Banking Maverick: Norwest Corp. Relies on Branches, Pushes Service—and Prospers," *Wall Street Journal*, August 17, 1995, A1.

Chapter 26

1. There are literally scores of studies on this fundamental topic. See, for instance, Richard Freeman and James Medoff, *What Do Unions Do?* (New York: Free Press, 1984); Dale Belman and Paula B. Voos, "Changes in Union Wage Effects by Industry: A Fresh Look at the Evidence," *Industrial Relations* 43 (July 2004): 491–519; Alison L. Booth and Mark L. Bryan, "The Union Membership Wage-Premium Puzzle: Is There a Free Rider Problem?" *Industrial and Labor Relations Review* 57 (April 2004): 402–421.

2. Freeman and Medoff, *What Do Unions Do?*

3. For instance, Steve G. Allen, "Unionization and Productivity in Office Building and School Construction," *Industrial and Labor Relations Review* 39 (1986), 187–201; Steven G. Allen, "The Effect of Unionism on Productivity in Privately and Publicly Owned Hospitals and Nursing Homes," *Journal of Labor Research* 7 (1986): 59–68.

4. Jeffrey Pfeffer and Jerry Ross, "Unionization and Income Inequality," *Industrial Relations* 20 (Fall 1981): 272–285.

5. See, for example, Jeffrey Pfeffer and Nancy Langton, "The Effect of Wage Dispersion on Satisfaction, Productivity, and Working Collaboratively: Evidence from College and University Faculty," *Administrative Science Quarterly* 38 (1993): 382–407; Matt Bloom, "The Performance Effects of Pay Dispersion on Individuals and Organizations," *Academy of Management Journal* 42 (1999): 25–40; and Phyllis A. Siegel and Donald C. Hambrick, "Pay Disparities Within Top Management Groups: Evidence of Harmful Effects on Performance of High Technology Firms," *Organizatonal Science* 16 (2005): 259–274.

6. Jeffrey Pfeffer and Jerry Ross, "Unionization and Female Wage and Status Attainment," *Industrial Relations* 20 (1981): 179–185.

7. See, for instance, Robert Drago, "Quality Circle Survival: An Exploratory Analysis," *Industrial Relations* 27 (1988): 336–351.

8. Ann Page (ed.), *Keeping Patients Safe: Transforming the Work Environment of Nurses* (Washington, DC: National Academies Press, 2004).

9. Michael Ash and Jean Ann Seago, "The Effect of Registered Nurses' Unions on Heart-Attack Mortality," *Industrial and Labor Relations Review* 57 (April 2004): 422–442.

10. Mark Schoeff, Jr., "Cingular, Union Strike a Tone of Cooperation," *Workforce Management*, July 2006, 12.

Chapter 27

1. Joann S. Lublin and Scott Thurm, "Money Rules: Behind Soaring Executive Pay, Decades of Failed Restraints," *Wall Street Journal*, October 13, 2006, A1.

2. Ibid.

3. Ibid.

4. Dan R. Dalton, Chatermine M. Daily, Allen E. Esstrand, and Jonathan L. Johnson, "Meta-analytic Reviews of Board Composition, Leadership Structure, and Financial Performance," *Strategic Manage-*

ment Journal 19 (1998): 269–290; see also David F. Larcker, Scott A. Richardson, and Irem Tuna, "Does Corporate Governance Really Matter?" working paper, Wharton School, University of Pennsylvania.

5. See, for instance, Charles A. O'Reilly, Brian G. M. Main, and Graef S. Crystal, "CEO as Tournament and Social Comparison: A Tale of Two Theories," *Administrative Science Quarterly* 33 (1988): 257–274.

6. Bengt Holmstrom, "*Pay Without Performance* and the Managerial Power Hypothesis: A Comment," *Journal of Corporation Law* (Summer 2005): 703–715.

7. Graef Crystal, *In Search of Excess* (New York: W. W. Norton, 1991).

8. Chuck Lucier, Rob Schuyt, and Edward Tse, "CEO Succession 2004: The World's Most Prominent Temp Workers," *Strategy + Business* 39 (Summer 2005), http://www.strategy-business.com/16239054/16927070.

9. "Global CEO Turnover Sets New Record in 2005, Booz Allen Hamilton Study Finds," press release, May 18, 2006.

10. Lublin and Thurm, "Money Rules," A16.

11. Jeffrey Pfeffer and Robert I. Sutton, *Hard Facts, Dangerous Half-Truths, and Total Nonsense: Profiting from Evidence-Based Management* (Boston: Harvard Business School Press, 2006), chapter 8.

12. Rakesh Khurana, *Searching for a Corporate Savior* (Princeton, NJ: Princeton University Press, 2002).

13. Holmstrom, "*Pay Without Performance* and the Managerial Power Hypothesis: A Comment."

Chapter 28

1. http://www.academicintegrity.org/cai_research.asp, August 19, 2006.

2. See, for instance, Donald L. McCabe and Linda Klebe Trevino, "Cheating Among Business Students: A Challenge for Business Leaders and Educators," *Journal of Management Education* 19 (May 1995): 205–218; Anne Hendershott, Patrick Drinan, and Megan Cross, "Toward Enhancing a Culture of Academic Integrity," *NASPA Journal* 37 (Summer 2000): 587–597.

3. B. F. Skinner, *Science and Human Behavior* (New York: Macmillan, 1953).

4. http://www.academicintegrity.org/cai_research.asp, August 19, 2006.

Index

"above-average effect," 184
absenteeism, 64
Accenture, 119
accidents in workplace, 70–71
accounting fraud, 189
Ackerloff, George, 8
adaptability of strategy, 170
Advisory Board, 154–155
AES, 36, 118–119
Aetna U.S. Healthcare, 59
Airbus, 52, 53, 71–72
Air Canada, 124
airline industry. *See also individual airlines*
   customer service horror stories, 116–117, 121
   "day in the field" programs, 118, 119
   lack of individuality in, 154
   layers of management in, 34
   problems in, 158
   role of pilots in cost savings, 54
   service-oriented culture, 16
   standout organizations in, 155–156
   success of "low-cost" airlines, 51–52
   wages and benefits, 49–50, 52
Alaska Airlines, 13, 51, 52
Albertsons, 49
Allen, Woody, 132
Amazon.com, 32
American Airlines, 34, 49–50, 151–152
American Express, 142
American Management Association (AMA), 63, 64
American Vantage, 97
Angus Reid Group, 62
AOL-Time Warner merger, 162
apparel industry, 50–51
Apple Computer, 105, 170, 186, 189
Asia, 175
association with powerful people, 97, 98, 99–100
A.T. Kearney, 27
Austin Hayne, 129
authority, "day in the field" programs and, 120

automated customer service software, 14–15
automobile industry, 52

BA (British Airways), 155
Bach, Johann Sebastian, 39
Baldrige quality award, 30–31, 97
Ballmer, Steve, 90
Banco Bilbao, 72
Bartlett, Eric, 40
Bauch, Ronnie, 39, 41, 42, 43
Bausch & Lomb, 88
Bed Bath & Beyond, 160
behavioral interviewing, 92
Belgium, 27
benchmarking
    as common practice, 154–155
    in performance assessment, 146
    in setting executive pay, 184
benefit plan management, 56–61
    defined contribution plans, 56–58
    role in hiring and recruitment of talent, 57, 60–61
    specialization and, 57, 58–59
Berkshire Partners, 152
best value proposition, 7
Bethune, Gordon, 169
Beyond Budgeting (Hope and Fraser), 142
Beyond Budgeting Round Table, 141

Blank, Arthur, 128–129
boards of directors, 181–182, 183
Boeing, 52, 71–72
Bradford, David, 22
Brenneman, Greg, 169
British Airways (BA), 155
Brocade Communications, 189
Brooks, Randy, 50
Brown, Tina, 104
Brown, Willie, 128
budgetary targets, 141–146
    attempts to meet, 143–145
    cutting training costs to meet, 176–177
    effort expended on budgets, 142–143
    ethical issues, 143–144
    performance assessment contrasted, 145–146
    problems caused by budgets, 141–142
Buffett, Warren, 112
Bush, George W., 102, 103, 107, 108
Business 2.0, 1–2
business press, 185–186
Business Roundtable, 185
business schools. *See also individual schools*
    academic integrity and, 190
    in Spain, 19–21
buzzwords, 167–168

Callaghan, Kevin, 152
call centers, 117

Canada, 124
  education in, 28
  global competitiveness of, 27
  hiring and recruitment,
    90–91
  incentive systems in, 76
  trade surpluses, 50
Canals, Jordi, 21
Canon, 169
career ambitions, self-promo-
    tion and, 95–101
Carlzon, Jan, 16
Carol Franc Buck Breast Care
    Center, 134–135
Carter, Jimmy, 99, 128
celebrity status of CEOs, 186,
    187
Cendant, 189
Center for Academic Integrity,
    191
Cerner, 69
Chakrabarty, Sanjay, 130–131
Challenger disaster, 123
change efforts, excuses and,
    134
channel stuffing, 144
Charles Schwab, 142
Chartered Institute of Person-
    nel and Development, 64
cheating, among college stu-
    dents, 189, 190–191
chief executive officers
    (CEOs). *See also* senior
    executives
  belief in importance of,
    185–186
  conformity pressures on, 163

executive pay, 181–187
  firings, 175, 184–185
Childtime Learning Centers,
    54–55
China, 28, 29, 50, 113
Christensen, Clayton, 106
Cialdini, Robert, 109
Cingular Wireless, 179–180
Clarke, Bill, 17
Clubb, Kathryn, 119
Colgate-Palmolive Company,
    112
colleges, cheating in, 189,
    190–191
Collins, Jim, 95
commitment, engagement and,
    42
common mistakes. *See* learning
    from mistakes; mistakes
communication
  of corporate values and cul-
    ture, 80
  emphasis on "sounding
    smart," 167–168
  framing and repetition in,
    102–108
  in member-centric organi-
    zations, 42–43
Communication Workers of
    America, 179–180
community, organization as,
    19–24
Compaq, 162, 165
comparative advantage, in
    assumption of risk, 60, 61
competition
  on basis of labor costs, 176

competition (*continued*)
  from Japan, ignoring,
    169–170
competitive advantage
  achieving, with organized
    labor, 179–180
  in airline industry, 51–52
  questionable actions and, 193
  role of human capital in,
    28–29
  sustainable, strategy and, 168
  U.S. government regulation
    and, 25–26
  wage reductions and, 53
competitive challenges
  employee loyalty and, 54
  mergers and, 160–162, 165
competitive dynamics, under-
    standing, 29
competitiveness, of U.S. com-
    panies, 82–83
ComScore Networks, 62
Comverse Technology, 189
Conference Board, 28, 68
confidence, projecting,
    104–106
conformity pressures, on
    CEOs, 163
Conley, Frances K., 105
consulting firms
  on compensation plans, 78,
    184
  medical claims assistance, 59
  overemphasis on client pre-
    sentations, 167
  strategy consulting, 168
  on well-run companies, 158

Consumer Products Safety
    Commission, 26
The Container Store, 30
Continental Airlines, 13,
    116–117, 121, 169
"continuous improvement,"
    32–33
corporate culture
  caring communities, 19–24
  communicating, 80
  culture of truth-telling, 124,
    125–126
  experimentation, 170
  leader-centric, 44–45
  learning fostered in, 38
  no-excuses culture, 133–138
  shareholder-oriented, 148
corporate misdeeds, 188–194.
    See also ethics; legal lia-
    bility
  college cheating and,
    189–192
  few penalties for, 189,
    192–193
  maintaining high ethical stan-
    dards and, 193–194
  personal reputation and,
    188–189, 192–193
"corporate savior," new CEO as,
    185
Costco, 50
cost-cutting, 157
Council of Graduate Schools,
    29
courtesy, 109–115
  importance of personal
    contact, 111–112

lack of, as problem, 109–110
paying attention to others,
110–111
power of flattery, 113–114
sharing social identity, 113
creative-class index, 27, 73
creative people, 50
credibility
"day in the field" programs
and, 119–120
truth-telling and, 105
Crew, Rudy, 134, 136–137
CRM (customer relationship
management) software,
14–15
Crystal, Graef, 184
Culp, Larry, 113
cultural sensitivities, courtesy
and, 112–113
culture of helplessness, 125
customer loyalty
importance of, 14
incentive systems and, 74
outstanding service and,
158–159
as performance measure, 153
customer needs, meeting,
158–159
customer relationship management (CRM) software,
14–15
customer relationships, 13–18,
74
building, 15–16
data on customer service,
13–14
listening to customers, 170

role of employees in, 16–18
software for "managing,"
14–15
customer satisfaction
with "low-cost" airlines,
51–52
as performance measure,
145–146
customer service
excuses as ineffective
strategy, 124–125
horror stories, 13, 116–117,
121
meeting customer needs,
158–159
outstanding, examples of,
155–158
profitability and, 51–52
as proven ingredient for
success, 55
service-oriented culture, 16,
74
surveys on, 13–14, 16, 74
customer service culture, 16, 74

Daimler-Chrysler merger, 162
Dalgaard, Lars, 129–130
Danaher Corporation, 113
The Da Vinci Code (film), 19
Da Vita, 20, 80, 112
"day in the field" programs,
119, 120, 121
"town meetings," 125–126
Da Vita Village Network, 20
"day in the field" programs,
118–119, 120, 121

Daylin Corporation, 129
"death spiral," 5, 6, 144
deception, in instilling confidence, 106
decision making
  on benefits, complexity of, 58–59
  common mistakes in (*see* mistakes)
  facts and, 123
  importance of truth in, 123
  joint, in labor-management partnerships, 178–179, 180
deferred compensation, 84–85, 182
defined benefit retirement plans, 56–57, 81–82
defined contribution plans, 56–58
Definity Health, 57
Dell Computer, 165
Deloitte Consulting, 56, 71, 96, 97, 98
Delta Airlines, 49–50
Deming, W. Edwards, 79
Denmark, 27, 68
Dilbert cartoons, 3
direct experience, 116–121
  building credibility and, 119–120
  "day in the field" programs, 118–119, 120, 121
  difficulties with, 120
  need for, 116–117, 121
  problem solving and, 117–118, 120, 121

discounting, 144
Discovery Group, 85
distributed power model, 39–45
division of labor, 57, 58–59
Drexel Burnham, 192
Dubai, 124
due diligence, 92, 164
Dunne, Jimmy, 129
Dyer, Richard, 42

earnings distribution, unions and, 175
"earnings management," 143–144, 151
Eastman Kodak, 61
Edmondson, Amy, 33, 34, 35
education. *See also* training; *specific institutions*
  cheating, 189, 190–191
  on corporate values and culture, 80
  disadvantages of, 131–132
  ethics in, 189
  importance of infrastructure, 29
  incentive pay in, 77
  no-excuses culture in, 134
  role of, 2
  of U.S. workforce, 28–29
effective workplaces
  benefit cuts and, 81–86
  benefit plan management and, 56–61
  building trust, 62–67
  cost-cutting and, 49–55
  hiring practices, 87–92

incentive systems and, 74–80
long hours and, 68–73
efficiency
"day in the field" programs
and, 120
length of workweek and, 72
short-term, learning from
mistakes and, 36–37
specialization and, 57,
58–59
total cost reduction and, 53
"efficiency wages," 8
employee(s)
distrust of deferred compensation plans, 84–85
electronically monitored,
63–65
as "face of business," 13–18
importance to customer relationships, 17–18
personal use of company
resources, 62–63
responsibility for managing
benefits, 56–61
salaries of (*see* wages)
shifting risk to, 57, 60, 61
wage and benefit reductions,
49–55, 81–86
employee attitudes
electronic monitoring and,
64–65
toward working environment,
71, 73
employee engagement
cost savings and, 54
electronic monitoring and,
64–65

in member-centric organization, 42
wage reductions and, 53
employee loyalty, 22, 54
employee motivation
incentive systems and, 76–77
wage and benefit reductions
and, 54–55
employee productivity. *See* productivity
employee retention, 86, 153
energy industry, 71
Enron, 43–44, 92, 122, 180,
189
entrapment, electronic surveillance and, 66
entrepreneurship, persistence
and, 129–130, 132
envy, self-promotion and, 97,
100–101
ePolicy Institute, 63
Equal Employment Opportunity Commission, 26
error reporting, 35–36, 125
escalating commitment, in
mergers, 164
Esserman, Laura, 134–135,
136, 137–138
ethics. *See also* legal liability
corporate misdeeds, 188–194
emphasis on, 21–22
lying on resumes, 87–88
meeting budgetary targets
and, 143–144
Europe. *See also specific countries*
average wages in, 51
dismissals of CEOs, 175

Europe (*continued*)
  education in, 28
  incentive systems in, 76
  length of workweek in,
    68–69, 71–72
European Union, 26
"event studies," 149
excuses. *See also* no-excuses
    culture
  culture of helplessness and,
    125
  as ineffective strategy,
    124–125
executive ego, 162, 163, 193
executive pay, 181–187
  "above-average effect" and, 184
  components of, disclosing,
    182–183
  factors in setting, 183–184
  in private companies,
    186–187
  proposals for reform of,
    181–183
  reasons for rise in, 184–185
  wage differentials, 181
experimentation, culture of, 170
external benchmarks. *See*
    benchmarking
extrinsic incentive bias, 78–79

face-to-face meetings, 112–113
Fastech, 130
Fastow, Andrew, 122, 189
Federal Trade Commission, 26
Federated Department Stores,
  160

feedback effects
  of benefit cuts, 57, 83–84
  importance of considering, 3,
    4–6, 9
  second-order effects, 33
  union effects on wages, 174
Ferrazzi, Keith, 96–98, 99, 100,
    192
Ferrazzi Greenlight, 96, 97
Feynman, Richard, 123
"final 3 feet," 17–18
financial services industry, 16
Finland, 27, 28, 72
Fiorina, Carly, 162
firings, of CEOs, 175, 184–185
"five forces" model, 158
flattery, 110, 113–114
Fleetwood Mac, 122
Florida, Richard, 27, 73
Ford-Jaguar merger, 162
Ford Motor Company, 52,
    60–61, 142, 177
forecasting ability, rewarding,
    143
formal modeling, of feedback
    effects, 6
Fortune best places to work, 30,
    61, 86, 149
Fortune 500 companies, 96
Fortune 1000 companies,
    81–82
401(k) defined contribution
    plans, 84
framing and repetition,
    102–108
  defining criteria for success,
    103–104

establishing terms, 106–107
projecting clarity and confidence, 104–106
relentless repetition, 107–108
France, 68, 69, 112, 113, 181
Fraser, Robin, 142
"free-riding" problem, 40
Free Willy (film), 170
Frontier Airlines, 52
fundamental attribution error, 187

Gallup surveys, 68
Gartner Group, 15
Gates, Bill, 90
General Electric, 30, 145
General Motors, 7, 49, 52, 104, 165
Germany, 50, 68, 69
Gittell, Jody Hoffer, 34
Global Business Systems, 130
global competitiveness, 27
   ignoring competition from Japan, 169–170
   mathematical proficiency and, 28–29
Globalization Index (A.T. Kearney), 27
Goldman Sachs, 152
Goodnight, Jim, 67, 71
Google, 32, 44, 90
government regulation, decreasing, 25–26
Great Place to Work Institute, 149
grocery industry, 17, 49, 50

gross domestic product (GDP), 69
Grove, Andy, 106

Habitat for Humanity, 128
Hackman, J. Richard, 40
Hambrick, Donald, 162
Hanwha, 76
Harbour Report, 52
Harrah's Entertainment, 37, 91, 123, 124
harsh treatment, "forgetting," 99–100
Harvard Business School, 27, 33, 40, 91, 96, 97, 98, 102, 103, 185
Harvard University medical insurance study, 84
Hayward, Matthew, 162
HCI (Human Capital Index), 149
health, 70, 84
Health Advocate, 59
health care, 58–59, 70
health care industry
   coming demographic crunch, 71
   error reporting in, 35–36, 125
   layers of management in, 34
   learning and implementation in, 33–34
   learning by doing in, 37
   no-excuses culture in, 134–135, 136
   positive effects of unionization on, 177–179

health care industry (*continued*)
reduced benefits and, 82
health insurance
customer service nightmares,
117
feedback effects in, 84
medical claims assistance, 59
for retirees, reductions in, 81
HealthSouth, 189
Hearst Corporation, 5–6
Heilemann, John, 111
Hewitt Associates, 75–76
Hewlett-Packard, 143–144, 162
Hewlett-Packard-Compaq
merger, 165
high-commitment work
arrangements, 176–177
high-performance work
practices, 176–177
hiring and recruitment, 87–92
automation of hiring process,
17
customer relationships and,
16–17
due diligence in, 92
ethics of lying on resumes,
87–88
investment in, 54–55
relevant information in, 89,
90–91
resume-processing software,
88–89
role of benefit plans in, 57,
60–61
role of interview in, 89–90,
92
Holmstrom, Bengt, 184, 186

The Home Depot, 129
home improvement industry, 17
Honda, 117–118, 121
honor codes, 190
Hope, Jeremy, 142
hospitality industry, 16
hospitals, 33–34
hostile work environment, 67
human behavior
adherence to simplistic
theories of (*see* simplistic
theories)
consequences of, 189–192
human capital, competitive
advantage and, 28–29
Human Capital Index (HCI),
149
human resource management,
173–174

IBM, 83–84, 105, 169
IBM Retirement Funds, 84
Iceland, 27
IDC Research, 62
IDEO, 37, 170
IESE, 68
caring culture of, 19–21
emphasis on ethics and values, 21–22
ImClone, 189
imitation, problems with, 155
immigration, 29
implementation, strategic planning and, 168
inAssist, 59
incentives and punishments, 7

incentive systems, 74–80
  employee motivation and,
    76–77
  examples of problems with,
    74–75, 79
  extrinsic incentive bias and,
    78–79
  performance measurement
    and, 77–78
  popularity of, 75–76
  proper use of, 79–80
income smoothing, 143–144
India, 28, 29, 113
individual interests, 95–96
individual pay for performance.
  See incentive systems
individual responsibility, 40–41,
  42
industrial psychology, 17
industry conditions, performance and, 158
influence. *See also* power
  building, through human
    interaction, 109–115
  social influence, executive
    pay and, 184
*Influence: The Psychology of
  Persuasion* (Cialdini), 109
Informix, 189, 192
innovation, capacity for, 31
The Innovation Group (TIG),
  22, 23
Innovation Index (global), 27
inspiration, persistence and,
  130
Institute of Management and
  Administration, 88

Institute of Medicine, 177
Institutional Shareholder
  Services, 88
Intel, 106
Intel Capital, 131
intellectual excitement of mergers, 162–163
intellectual skill, 127
intentional sabotage, 4, 5
International Labour Office, 69
Internet, cheating and, 191
interviews, 89–90, 92
investment bankers, 162–163
investments
  in hiring and recruitment,
    54–55
  long-term, short-term budget
    targets and, 144–145
  in overseas R&D, 28
investor relations, 152
investor relations departments,
  147–148
investor relations professionals,
  149
Iraq war, 108
Ireland, 27, 51
Italy, 50–51, 69

Japan
  average wages in, 51
  education in, 28
  global competitiveness of, 27
  ignoring competition from,
    169–170
  incentive systems in, 76
  investor relations in, 148

Japan (*continued*)
  length of workweek in, 69
  trade surplus with China, 50
  wage differentials in, 181
Jerry Maguire (film), 84–85
JetBlue, 50, 51, 53, 54
job dissatisfaction, 50
Jobs, Steve, 90, 105, 186
Johnson, Lyndon B., 100, 111,
  114
Jordan, Michael, 58

Kaiser-Permanente Medical
  Group, 178–179
Kansas City Southern, 158
Kearns, David, 169–170
Kenexa, 17
Kerry, John, 107
Khurana, Rakesh, 44, 185
Kissinger, Henry, 100
Kmart, 152
"knowing-doing" gap, 14
knowledge work, 28, 72–73
Korea, 76, 188
Kotter, John, 103
Kovacevich, Richard, 108, 169
Kroger, 49
Kronos, 17
Kumar, Ram, 88

labor costs
  competition on basis of, 176
  components of, 53
  economizing on, unions and,
    174–175
  total costs and, 53
  wage rates contrasted, 50, 52
labor-management partner-
  ships, 178–179, 180
labor productivity, unions and,
  175
labor shortage, coming, 61, 71,
  73
Lampert, Edward, 152
language of discussion, control
  of, 106–107
Larcker, David, 142
Lauer, Matt, 104
Lay, Kenneth, 43, 122
layoffs, 144, 177
leader-centric organization,
  41–42
  corporate culture, 44–45
  problems with, 43–44
  as traditional model, 40
"leaderless organization," 39
leadership. *See also* influence;
  power
  building influence through
    interaction, 109–115
  executive ego and, 162, 163,
    193
  familiarity with daily opera-
    tions, 116–121
  framing and repetition in,
    102–108
  making excuses and,
    133–138
  persistence and, 127–132
  self-promotion and, 95–101
  truth, importance of,
    122–126

leadership development, 44–45
leadership skills
  character, 91–92
  listening as, 41–42
leading by example, 137–138
learning from mistakes, 32–38
  emphasis on innovation,
    32–33
  error reporting and, 35–36
  finding and fixing problems,
    33–36
  layers of management and,
    34–35
  short-term efficiency and,
    36–37
"learning organization," 32–33
Lee, Fiona, 124
legal liability. *See also* corporate
    misdeeds; ethics
  age discrimination suits, 84
  employee monitoring and,
    63–64
  for libel, resumes and, 89
  mandatory error reporting
    and, 125
Lehman Brothers, 152
leisure, quality of life and, 69
L.E.K. Consulting, 150
Les Schwab Tire Centers,
    158–159
Lev, Baruch, 150–151
leveraged buyout (LBO) trans-
    actions, 152
Levi Strauss, 51
Levitt, Steve, 77
life insurance, for retirees,
    reductions in, 81

Lincoln Award for Business
    Excellence, 97
listening, 41–42
lobbying efforts, 111
Loconto, Pat, 98
Lonchar, Ken, 88
long-term investments,
    144–145
Los Angeles Times, 5
Loveman, Gary, 91, 123, 124
"low-cost" airlines, 51–52
Lowe's, 17
loyalty
  customer loyalty, 14, 74, 153,
    158–159
  employee loyalty, 22, 54

Mackey, John, 157
Macy's, 160
Macy's West, 117
The Mailroom (Rensin), 99
Malcolm Baldrige National
    Quality Award (MBNQA),
    30–31, 97
management
  human capital management,
    software for, 129, 141
  human resource management,
    unions and, 173–174
  labor-management partner-
    ships, 178–179, 180
  layers of, 34–35
  people management, norm of
    reciprocity in, 8–9
  scientific management
    movement, 117

management (*continued*)
  self-managed teams, 44
  total quality management, 32,
    37, 177
management approaches
  disciplined, length of work-
    week and, 72
  nurturing social inclinations,
    23–24
  organization as caring culture,
    19–24
management consensus, as
  problem, 165
mandatory error reporting, 125
manufacturing sector, 53, 71,
  73
Marcus, Bernard, 128–129
Mark, Reuben, 112
Martin, Roger, 90–91
Massachusetts Institute of
  Technology (MIT), 6
mathematical proficiency,
  28–29
May Company, 160
MBNQA (Malcolm Baldrige
  National Quality Award),
  30–31, 97
McCabe, Don, 189, 190
McCall, Morgan, 45
MCG Capital, 88
McKinsey & Company, 98
McNealy, Scott, 167
McQuilling, Andrew, 112
measures of success
  creating standout organi-
    zation, 154–159
  hype about strategy, 166–170

resisting pressures to merge,
  160–165
shareholder return, 147–153
tyranny of budget and,
  141–146
media business, 5–6
medical claims assistance, 59
medical insurance. *See* health
  insurance
medicine, unionization in, 177
meetings, face-to-face,
  112–113
member-centric organization,
  39–45
  communication in, 42–43
  costs of, 43
  engagement in, 42
  example of, 39–40, 41
  job satisfaction in, 40–41
  skill-building in, 41–42
  "wisdom of crowds" in, 43–44
Men's Wearhouse, 79
  "day in the field" programs,
    118–119, 120, 121
  as standout company,
    156–157
  training, 30, 31
mental health, 70
mergers, avoiding, 160–165
  excitement of mergers and,
    162–163
  executive ego and, 162, 163
  failed mergers, 161, 164
  operational problems and,
    160–162
  principle of scarcity and,
    163–164

Merrill Lynch, 135–136
Miami-Dade County schools, 134
Microsoft Corporation, 71, 90
Milken, Michael, 192–193
Milliken, 30
Milton, Robert, 124
mistakes, 1–10
    admitting, importance of, 124–125
    customer-service mistakes, 116–117
    error reporting, 35–36, 125
    feedback effects, failure to consider, 3, 4–5
    learning from (*see* learning from mistakes)
    long working hours and, 70–71
    overcomplication, 3, 8–9
    overview, 1–3
    simplistic theories, adherence to, 3, 6–8
    trial and error, 170
MIT (Massachusetts Institute of Technology), 6
Mitchell, Bryan J., 88
MobiApps, 130–131
Money magazine, 158
Monitor, 90–91
monopoly, effects of unions on, 174
morality, of benefit cuts, 82, 83
Motion Picture Association of America (MPAA), 111
Motorola, 30–31
Motorola University, 30

MTW, 22–23
Mulcahy, Anne, 125
"multileader organization," 39–45
"multitasking," as discourteous, 109–110, 114–115

National Association of Corporate Directors, 168
National Football League, 101
National Investor Relations Institute, 149
National Labor Relations Board, 26
NBC network, 104
Netherlands, 27, 28
networking, 97
newspaper business, 5–6
New York City schools, 134
The New Yorker, 104
New York Philharmonic, 40
New York Times, 5–6
Nike, 51, 170
Nishimura, Ko, 78
Nobel Peace Prize, 128
no-excuses culture, 133–138
    articulating vision of, 136–137
    examples of, 134–135
    excuses made by senior executives, 133–134
    leading by example, 137–138
    prevalence of excuse-making, 133–134
    refusal to allow excuses, 135–136

"noisy complainers," 34
Nokia, 72
Nordstrom, 17
norms of reciprocity, 8–9, 31,
    184
North America, 175
North American International
    Auto Show, 104
Northwest Airlines, 49–50,
    119, 155
Norway, 27
Norwest, 108
Nvidia, 150

OECD (Organisation for Eco-
    nomic Co-operation and
    Development), 27
Opus Dei, 19–20
Oracle, 165
O'Reilly, Charles, 184
organization(s)
    as caring culture, 19–24
    labor unions, 173–180
    "leaderless organization," 39
    "learning organization," 32–33
    member-centric, 39–45
    outstanding, 154–159
organizational interests, 95–96
organizational learning, 32–38
organizational success, 7
organized labor, 173–180
    achieving competitive advan-
        tage with, 179–180
    effect on wage inequality,
        175–176
    effect on wages, 174–175

high-performance work prac-
    tices and, 176–177
positive effects of, in
    medicine, 177–179
seen as anachronism,
    173–174
Orpheus Chamber Orchestra,
    39–40, 41, 42, 45
Orr, Kelly, 50
Ossie, Ed, 22–23
ostracism, 23
outcomes, error reporting and,
    35
outsourcing, 130
outstanding organizations,
    154–159
    airline industry example,
        155–156
    benchmarking and, 154–155
    grocery industry example,
        157–158
    meeting customer needs and,
        158–159
    retailing sector example,
        156–157
overcomplication, 3, 8–9, 78
overconfidence, in mergers, 164

Page, Larry, 90
Patagonia, 44
Pathmark Supermarkets, 54
Patterson, Neal, 69
pay for performance. *See* incen-
    tive systems
peer acceptance, cheating and,
    191

people-centered strategies
customer relationships,
13–18
learning from mistakes,
32–38
"multileader" organizations,
39–45
organization as caring community, 19–24
training, 25–31
Peopleclick, 133
people management, 8–9
PeopleSoft, 165
performance
compared to budget, 142
executive pay not tied to,
181, 186
high-performance work practices, 176–177
individual pay for (*see* incentive systems)
industry conditions and, 158
of "low-cost" airlines, 51–52
rewarding forecasting ability
and, 143
self-confidence and, 31
performance appraisal software,
129
performance criteria, defining,
103–104
performance indicators, 145
performance measurement, 153
customer satisfaction as,
145–146
incentive systems and, 77–78
stock price as, inaccuracy of,
150–151

persistence, 127–132
commitment to, 130–131
entrepreneurship and,
129–130, 132
success and, 128–129
personal charm, influence and,
109–115
personal contact
courtesy and, 111–112
importance of, 112–113
personal relationships, 22, 24,
183
personal reputation, 188–189,
192–193
personal use of company
resources, 62–63
Peter Principle, 90
Petersen, Donald, 177
Pew Charitable Trusts, 14, 15
Pfeffer, Kathleen, 20–21, 74
Pixar Animation Studios, 105
placebo effect, 106
political strategies, 102–108,
128
Porter, Michael, 27, 158
power. *See also* influence
association with powerful
people, 97, 98, 99–100
distributed power model,
39–45
ethical issues, 193
exercising, framing, and repetition in, 102–108
power of flattery, 113–114
PowerPoint presentations, 167,
170
"practical smarts," 131–132

presentations, slick, 166–167
PricewaterhouseCoopers, 73, 83
principle of scarcity, 163–164
private companies, 186–187
problems
    caused by budgets, 141–142
    imitation as, 155
    with incentive systems, 74–75, 79
    lack of courtesy as, 109–110
    with leader-centric organizations, 43–44
    learning from mistakes, 33–36
    management consensus as, 165
    operational, mergers and, 160–162
    refusal to admit, mergers and, 163
    surfacing, 122, 123
problem solving
    direct experience and, 117–118, 120, 121
    finding and fixing root causes, 33–34, 79
Procter & Gamble, 170
productivity
    advantages of unions to, 175
    labor costs and, 53
    length of workweek and, 69–70, 73
productivity growth
    "buying" with mergers, 161–162
    in European Union, 26

training and, 30–31
"professional sons," 100
psychological bases of self-promotion, 98–100
psychological commitment, 99
psychological principle of scarcity, 163–164
psychological reactance, 7, 65
public companies
    executive pay in, 185
    going private, 152–153, 186
    strategies of, 168
public policy, 82
public sector, 71
Putnam Toyota, 74

quality, success and, 55
quality of life, leisure and, 69
"quick fix," incentive systems as, 79

Raley's, 17
Rayburn, Sam, 100
R&D (research and development), 28
Reagan, Ronald, 128
"Reality 101" program, 119
"reality distortion field," 105
reciprocity norms, 8–9, 31, 184
Recruit, 76
recruitment. *See* hiring and recruitment
Regan, Donald, 135–136
Regent Hotel, 119

rejection, learning to deal with, 42–43
relationship-building skills, 111–114
   consistent courtesy, 111–112
   customers and (*see* customer relationships)
   in-person meetings, 112–113
   power of flattery, 113–114
   sharing social identity, 113
reliability, as measurement criterion, 150
Repenning, Nelson, 6
research and development (R&D), 28
resilience, 128–129, 132
resource allocation, 145–146
ResumeDoctor.com, 87–88
resume-processing software, 88–89
resumes, 87–92
   due diligence and, 92
   interviews and, 89–90, 92
   lack of relevant information on, 89, 90–91
   misstatements on, 87–88
Resumix, 88
retailing sector
   automated hiring in, 17
   example of outstanding organization, 156–157
   problems in, 158
   service-oriented culture, 16
retirement
   complexity of decisions on, 58–59
   rejecting, 83–84

retirement benefits
   as deferred compensation, 84–85
   defined benefit plans, 56–57, 81–82
   reduced, 81–84
retirement seminars, 59
Rich, Jim, 84
Ricoh, 169
rigidity in strategy, 169–170
risk, shifting to employees, 57, 60, 61
risk-taking, in self-promotion, 96–97, 98
Rogers Commission, 123
Rotman Business School, 90–91
Russell, Richard, 100
Russo, David, 133–134

Safeway, 49
Saks Fifth Avenue, 144
salaries. *See* executive pay; wages
sales, emphasis on, 156–157
sales commissions, 74
Sall, John, 168
Sandler O'Neill, 129
San Francisco Chronicle, 5–6
SAP, 165
Saratoga Institute, 154–155
SAS Institute, 6, 67, 71, 73, 85–86, 133, 168
Satre, Phil, 91
Saturn, 177
Scandinavian countries. *See also specific countries*

Scandinavian countries
(*continued*)
global competitiveness of, 27
index of creative work, 73
scarcity, principle of, 163–164
scenario analysis, 6
Schönberg, Arnold, 39
Schwarzenegger, Arnold,
177–178
scientific management movement, 117
Sears Holdings, 152
Sears Roebuck & Co., 152
second-order feedback effects,
33
Securities and Exchange Commission (SEC), 183
selection science, 17
selective memory, 99, 100
self-confidence, 31, 104–106
"self-delusion," in mergers, 164
self-enhancement bias, 162
self-enhancement motive,
113–114
self-fulfilling prophecies,
65–66, 105
self-labeling, 65
self-managed teams, 44
self-promotion, 95–101
individual versus organizational interests, 95–96
networking and, 97
personal trade-offs in,
100–101
risk taking in, 96–97, 98
sound psychological bases of,
98–100

senior executives
ability to make excuses,
133–134
bluffing by, 125–126
CEOs (*see* chief executive
officers)
culture of truth-telling and,
124, 125
direct experience and,
116–121
executive ego and, 162, 163,
193
information filtered to,
122–123
salaries of (*see* executive pay)
stock options for, 77
service-oriented culture, 16, 74
SexTracker, 62
shareholder-oriented business
culture, 148
shareholder return. *See* total
shareholder return (TSR)
shareholder value, mergers and,
161
Shelton, Henry, 167
short-termism, 149–150
Silicon Valley Manufacturing
Group, 25
similarity, attraction and,
119–120
simplistic theories, adherence
to, 3, 6–8
Singapore, 27, 130–131
Singapore Airlines, 51–52,
155–156
SK Corporation, 188
SK Global, 188

Skilling, Jeff, 122, 189
Skinner, B. F., 189
slacking, 4, 5
Sloan, Alfred, 165
Sloan program (Stanford), 129
small experiments, in learning,
37
Smith, Adam, 58
social comparison, executive
pay and, 183, 187
social identity, sharing, 113
social inclinations, nurturing,
23–24
social influence, executive pay
and, 184
social isolation, 23
social sanctions, for white-
collar crime, 193
Society for Human Resource
Management, 88
software
CRM software, 14–15
to electronically monitor
employees, 63–65
human capital management,
129, 141
Internet-based cheating and,
191
problems with, finding and
fixing, 33–34
resume-processing software,
88–89
software industry, 117
Solectron, 53, 78
Southwest Airlines, 7, 50, 152,
156, 158
caring culture of, 21

competitive success of, 51
customer relationships, 16
"day in the field" program,
118, 121
layers of management, 34
successful strategy of,
168–169
unionized, 179
wage rates, 52
Spain, 19–21, 68, 72, 181
specialization, 57, 58–59
Spetzler, Carl, 135
Spitzer, Eliot, 128
Spurrier, Steve, 101
SRI International, 135
staff reductions, 144
standardized testing, 92
Stanford Business School, 39,
129, 133, 190
Stanford Medical School, 105
Stanford Shopping Center, 144
Stanford University, 90, 96,
127, 142
honor code of, 190
response to unethical behavior of students, 191–192
retirement seminars, 59
Starwood Hotels, 96, 98
status
celebrity status of CEOs,
186, 187
as "contagious," 100
out-of-touch executives and,
118
Sterman, John, 6
Stewart, Martha, 189, 192
stock market analysts, 148

stock options, 77, 189
stock price. *See also* total share-
    holder return (TSR)
    as inaccurate measure of per-
        formance, 150–151
    unanticipated changes and,
        151–152
Strategic Decisions Group, 135
strategy(ies), 166–170
    emphasis on presentations,
        166–167
    ineffective, excuses as,
        124–125
    issue of performance targets
        and, 146
    people-centered (*see* people-
        centered strategies)
    political, 102–108, 128
    rigidity in, 169–170
    simple, success of, 168–169
    talk versus action, 167–168
stress, 24, 65, 70
strong-leader organization. *See*
    leader-centric organization
success, 7
    competitive success, 51–52
    defining criteria for, 103–104
    measuring (*see* measures of
        success)
    persistence and, 128–129
    role of quality and customer
        service, 55
    of simple strategies, 168–169
Success Factors, 127, 129–130
Sun Hydraulics, 44
Sun Microsystems, 167

sustainable competitive
    advantage, 168
Sutton, Bob, 34, 165
Svenska Handelsbanken, 141
Sweden, 27
Switzerland, 27

Taiwan, 27
Talk magazine, 104
Target, 160
taxation, 26–27, 182
Taylor, Frederick Winslow, 117
TDIndustries, 30
technology
    customer relationship
        management, 14–15
    resume-processing software,
        88–89
Texans Credit Union, 59
Thiry, Kent, 112, 125–126
3i (venture capital firm), 131
Tiedens, Larissa, 124
TIG (The Innovation Group),
    22, 23
time
    spent on benefit plans, 57, 59
    spent on investor relations,
        148, 152
Time magazine, 19
Time Warner, 1–2, 162
Today Show, 104
total quality management, 37,
    177
total quality management
    movement, 32

total shareholder return (TSR), 147–153
avoiding market pressures and, 152–153
"earnings management" and, 151
investor relations departments and, 147–148
as measure of company quality, 148–149
obsession with, problem of, 149–150
reliability of, 150
validity of, 150–151
Towers Perrin, 85
"town meetings," 125–126
Toyota, 7, 52
Toyota 101, 74
trade surplus, wages and, 50–51
training, 25–31. *See also* education
benefits of, 30–31, 157–158
costs of, responsibility for, 29–30
as easily-cut budget item, 176–177
expenditures on, 32
harsh treatment during, 99–100
persistence and, 130
Trevino, Linda, 189, 190
trial and error, 170
Tribune Company, 5
Troupe, Quincy, 88
trust, 62–67

deferred compensation and, 84–86
electronic monitoring of employees and, 63–67
employee turnover and, 86
personal use of company resources and, 62–63
shared experiences and, 119–120
truth, 122–126
admitting mistakes, 124–125
credibility and, 105
culture of truth-telling, 124, 125–126
executives insulated from, 122–123
importance in decision making, 123
instilling confidence and, 105–106
as problem in mergers, 164
TSR. *See* total shareholder return (TSR)
Tufte, Edward, 167
turmoil caused by mergers, 164–165
Turnitin.com, 191
turnover
deferred compensation and, 84
low, employee trust and, 86
role of wages in, 4, 5, 53, 174
Tyco International, 92, 180
tyranny of budget, 141–146

UBS, 112
uncertainty
  reducing, by projecting confidence, 104–106
  turmoil and, in mergers, 164–165
Unicru, 17
unions. *See* organized labor
United Airlines, 13, 49–50, 156
  "cost disadvantage" of, 52, 53
  pilot slowdown, 54
United Auto Workers (UAW), 49, 177
United Healthcare, 57
United Kingdom, 14, 51, 64, 88, 181
United Parcel Service (UPS), 179
United Shareholders of America, 182–183
United States
  competitiveness of companies, 82–83
  global competitiveness of, 27
  loss of competitive advantage, 25–26
  trade deficit of, 51
  uneducated workforce in, 28–29
  working hours, 68, 69–70
University of California at San Francisco, 134–135
University of Florida, 101
University of Navarra, 19–21, 68
University of Toronto, 90–91

UPS (United Parcel Service), 179
U.S. Army, 91–92
U.S. Joint Chiefs of Staff, 167
US Airways, 49–50, 52

Valenti, Jack, 109–114
validity, as measurement criterion, 150–151
Value Line Investment Survey, 151–152
values, 21–22, 80
Vanity Fair, 104
Vault.com, 62
Veritas Software, 88
Virgin Atlantic Airways, 13, 51–52, 155–156
vision, articulating, 136–137

wage and benefit reductions, 49–55, 81–86. *See also* benefit plan management
  in airline industry, 49–54
  effects on competitiveness, 50–51
  employee motivation and, 54–55
  employee reactions to, 4, 5
  examples of, 49–50
  frozen retirement plans, 81–82
  labor rates versus labor costs, 52–53
  morality of, 82, 83

refusal to retire and, 83–84
total costs and, 53–54
trust and, 84–86
wage inequality, 175–176
wage rates, 50, 52, 53
wages
    effect of unions on, 174–175
    "efficiency wages," 8
    executive pay (*see* executive
        pay)
    feedback effects of cuts in,
        4–6
    growth of, training and,
        30–31
    pay for performance (*see*
        incentive systems)
    pay secrecy, 187
    survey data on, 75–76, 184
Wagoner, Rick, 104
Walgreens, 158
Walker, Lew, 179–180
Wal-Mart, 49, 50, 157, 158,
    160
Watkins, Sherron, 43–44,
    122
Watson Wyatt, 149
Welch, Jack, 107–108, 145
"welfare capitalism," 60
Wells Fargo Bank, N.A., 108
Wells Fargo & Co., 169
Wells Fargo-First Interstate
    Bank merger, 162
whistleblowing, 43–44
White, Phil, 192

white-collar crime. *See* cor-
    porate misdeeds
Whitney, John, 54
Whitworth, Ralph, 182–183
Whole Foods Market, 7, 17, 50,
    157–158
The Wisdom of Crowds
    (Surowiecki), 44
work samples, 92
"work to rule," 54
workweek, 68–73
    in Europe, 68–69, 71–72
    knowledge work and, 72–73
    mistakes and accidents,
        70–71
    productivity and, 69–70, 73
WorldCom, 92, 180, 189
World Economic Forum, 27
World Health Organization, 70
World Trade Center attacks,
    16, 108, 129
www.fakeresume.com, 88

Xerox Corporation, 125,
    169–170

Yahoo!, 37
YaYa Media, 96–97, 192

Zarrella, Ronald, 88
Zimmer, George, 79–80

Acknowledgments

This book came into being through a series of accidental events. In the fall of 2002, Josh Quittner, the new editor at *Business 2.0*, whom I had met at a dinner a few months previously, sent me an e-mail asking if I was interested in being a management columnist at the magazine.

As it turns out, I had actually wanted to be a columnist, mostly because I saw so much discussion in the press and on television of both corporate and world events that struck me as singularly uninformed by the research literature in organizational behavior and social psychology. And I saw lots of companies doing lots of things that made absolutely no sense based on that literature and on logical analysis.

So, I replied in the affirmative to Josh, and we agreed that I would give it a try. My first column ran in January 2003. As I write these acknowledgements, I am coming to the end of my fourth year as a columnist for *Business 2.0*—a long time in this game, I'm told, because columnists turn over regularly. I have loved every minute of it. The columns have given me the opportunity to interview some amazing people, to read more expansively than I would have ever done, to think about all kinds of interesting issues, to develop my writing skills under the best possible guidance, and to experience at least some aspects of the world of magazine publishing. But the columns are one page, which, when you put in the illustrations and the headline and the sub-headline and my brief biography, leaves me and my editors just 650 words. Although my editors have done a superbly fabulous job of keeping the essential content in each column, there is no question that this brevity causes things to be lost—the richness of more data and information, the ability to develop arguments a little more extensively, the ability to put in more, and more detailed, examples.

So, about a year ago I approached Quittner with a proposal: would he give me permission to use a selection of those columns as the foundation for a book in which I would take the original idea or theme and expand on it—not a lot, but just enough to provide more completeness and integrity to the analysis. He responded enthusiastically in the affirmative. This book is the result of the effort that ensued. In the process, I redid more than I anticipated, did more research than I had contemplated, and combined topics and reorganized the outline a few times. This process has, I hope, provided material that will be of use not only to leaders of companies and those who work in them but also to people who are interested in understanding the ins and outs of the organizational world.

Thanks for help with this book must begin with Josh Quittner, the first person to see a potential columnist where others saw a Stanford organizational behavior professor. And then, of course, many thanks to the magnificent, and I mean truly amazing, editors and fact checkers I have had the privilege of working with over the past four years. Some are rock musicians in their off-hours, some collect airplane parts, some have gone on to other careers in other Time Warner magazines or have left publishing, but all have been gracious and helpful. I have had the joy of working closely with Paul Sloan, Todd Lappin, Andy Raskin, Jeff Davis, Owen Thomas, and Eric Schurenberg, as well as numerous interns and fact checkers.

My writing and research benefits mightily from my Stanford colleagues. Special thanks to Bob Sutton for his insight, creativity, wisdom, and support—he is truly a special collaborator and a very special friend. Chip Heath provided a process for figuring out the title for this book and is a colleague who has always been a fan of the 2.0 columns and my attempt to write for both the academic and the managerial worlds. Charles O'Reilly has provided feedback on many ideas and continues to be a good friend and confidante. All of my colleagues in the organizational behavior group are just amazing—some of their work is cited in the text, and their insights and intelligence make me a better professor.

The people—practicing managers and leaders—who have given so generously of their time and insights or have permitted me to watch them do their thinking and their work are the real heroes of this book, even if sometimes their contributions to my writing and insights were a little inadvertent. These folks include George Zimmer, Colleen Barrett, David Kelley, Lars Dalgaard, Gary Loveman, Kent Thiry, Joe Mello, Bonny Warner Simi, George Parker, Chris Marsh, Kevin Goodwin, Jeff Miller, Anil Bhusri, Jack Valenti, Sanjay Chakrabarty, Keith Ferrazzi, Ronnie Bauch, Jim Franklin, Laurette Beeson, Roger Martin, Tim Tomlinson, Steve Ciesinski, Jack Watts, Jim Franklin, and David Kreps. Daphne Chang, who works in the Jackson Library at Stanford's Graduate School of Business, continues to provide simply outstanding levels of help and support when I can't find data or references, and has become an integral part of the work I do at Stanford.

This book also would not have come about without the efforts of my amazing agent, Don Lamm. He is not only an accomplished author's representative, he is also a friend and a wonderful human being. Melinda Merino at Harvard Business School Press, my editor on this project, never ceases to amaze me for her wisdom, patience, judgment, and just fabulous intelligence, good sense, and good will. She always understands what I am trying to do, sometimes better than I do, and has provided just the right mix of support and developmental criticism and thinking to help make the final product better and truer to its vision. She has been the perfect partner in this endeavor.

Something—this book—that arose in part because of luck and circumstance, cannot help but remind me of the profound role of chance in our lives. On a Saturday night some twenty-plus years ago, January 19, 1985, through a long chain of fortuitous and very unlikely circumstances, I was at a party where I met Kathleen F. Fowler. On July 23, 2006, we celebrated our 20th anniversary. Kathleen and I never cease to be amazed at how random events play such an important role in life. Chance played a role in my becoming a magazine columnist, and therefore, in writing this book. And it was pure chance that brought me the Amazing Kathleen, and all that has followed. This book is dedicated to her.

About the Author

JEFFREY PFEFFER is the Thomas D. Dee II Professor of Organizational Behavior at the Graduate School of Business, Stanford University, where he has taught since 1979. He is the author or coauthor of twelve books, including *The Human Equation: Building Profits by Putting People First*; *Managing with Power: Politics and Influence in Organizations*; *The Knowing-Doing Gap: How Smart Companies Turn Knowledge into Action*; *Hidden Value: How Great Companies Achieve Extraordinary Results with Ordinary People*; and *Hard Facts, Dangerous Half Truths, and Total Nonsense: Profiting from Evidence-Based Management*, as well as more than 110 articles and book chapters. Dr. Pfeffer received his BS and MS degrees from Carnegie-Mellon University and his PhD from Stanford. He began his career at the business school at the University of Illinois and then taught at the University of California, Berkeley. Pfeffer has been a visiting professor at the Harvard Business School, Singapore Management University, London Business School, and IESE in Barcelona.

Pfeffer currently serves on the board of directors of Audible Magic and SonoSite and writes a monthly column on management issues entitled "The Human Factor" for the 650,000-circulation *Business 2.0* magazine. He has presented seminars in 28 countries worldwide as well as doing consulting and providing executive education for numerous companies, associations, and universities in the United States.